What readers say abo

"The clearest message for me is: ˥
Today suggests gentle, effective wε
daily lives and help secure a briξ
the Earth that hosts us."

DEB HOY, Editor *Touch* Magazine. ⌣ι⌣
(available from www.reikiassociation.org.uk)

"Although *And I Saw a New Earth* is an extremely 'easy read', it is one I felt needed to be taken slowly and steadily to be able to fully digest all the fascinating and encouraging information within its pages. With each chapter being devoted to a particular subject, this book answers many questions whilst opening up new perspectives for the reader to explore. One of the best channelled works I have seen – it has certainly given me much on which to ponder."

JOAN OSBOURNE, Paradigm Shift Magazine March 2013

"The message in *Planet Earth Today* really resonated with me – it has helped open up a completely new way of thinking about the world we live in for me. Being a Reiki student, the messages about Reiki were particularly important for me – especially the benefits of having Reiki circles infused with joy."

MAMTA NANDA, Reiki Master UK

"Amazing account of Atlantis - as real as being there in flesh & blood! I love *The Downfall of Atlantis*! It made me feel so at home.[...]This book presents Atlantis as if you are physically there and going through its history day by day.[...]Once I opened the book I literally could not put it down and practically inhaled it. I could read it over and over again and it still feels fresh as if I've never read it before. I can't quite explain it and to be honest don't really want to. I just love it!"

M. BAYLES

"I was very inspired by *Guidebook to the Future!*... This book gives great insight into the new cycle that was started at that time and prepares us for the changes that may come in so many aspects of our lives. Having read it many months ago, I am surprised at how much there is still to learn from it. Not only is it worth reading, it is worth re-reading." K. TLUSTY-RISSMAN

"I've loved all of Candace's books; I've read each of them from start to finish with nothing more than a break for meals! Having tried on all religions for size only to find they don't sit well with me, I continued my search for truth, this is the closest I've come to it. *Stepping Through the Looking Glass* is a book I'll pick up when I need to feel inspired, and when I'm feeling less than charitable towards fellow human beings. It's a great read (all her books are) for anyone struggling to find compassion for others."
KAREN S.

"My experience of this book is that it comes at a time when it would be easy to fall into a deep depression about the state of the Earth; the craziness of humanity's behaviour, the collective mess we have made (which seems increasingly difficult to reverse), the proliferation of lies, 'fake news', an absence of trust and the veiling of truth.[...]If everybody could read and digest *After We Die* they would have a fresh perspective on the problem; with a much greater understanding of what is actually going on at the moment.[...]I particularly appreciated references to specific dates in recent times when significant Earth changes occurred; one can review events in one's own life that match the time frame and gain amazing insights as a result. Such details totally validated the content of this book. There is a lot of compassion and reassurance in these pages, something we all need more than ever."
HELEN CAMPBELL

Dawn of the Endless Day

Practical Steps for Living with the Earth and Hope for the Future

By Candace Caddick

Brightstone Publishing

First published 2022

Published by Brightstone Publishing
7 Blackstone Hill
Redhill, Surrey RH1 6BE
United Kingdom

ISBN registered to me, the author, under Brightstone Publishing.

British Library Cataloguing in Publication Data
A catalogue record for this book is available from the British Library

ISBN 978-0-9565009-6-0

Printed in the United Kingdom

Cover desrign ????/

Acknowledgements

I would like to thank my daughters Pippa and Heather Caddick for their unstinting support for me while writing this book. I'm also grateful for the encouragement and help from my friends Karen Jones and Grainne Warner. Support comes in different forms and practising the ideas and information in this book with my Earth Magic Healing Group online community has brought the pages to life for me; I'm indebted to Grainne and everyone in the group.

Books by Candace Caddick

"Do your little bit of good where you are; it's those little bits of good put together that overwhelm the world."
Archbishop Desmond Tutu

Contents

Foreword

This book was written during the Covid-19 pandemic. There was a desire on the part of Archangel Melchizadek to explain the pandemic and its place in the human timeline here on Earth. Ultimately, the pandemic's role was to create the emotional capacity in humanity to deal with death as well as being a harbinger of events to come.

By 2020 humanity had a pretty good understanding that the Earth was being exploited in an unsustainable fashion. Despite this understanding, it seemed impossible for the changes to be made to stop activity harmful to the planet and begin repairing it on behalf of all life here. The year 2020 was the first of a five-year period where the way of living for humanity would be wrenched out of its current pathway and reset on one with a sustainable future.

For this to happen, according to the Archangel Melchizadek, we would have events to force change. First up was the global Covid pandemic. Covid would bring death out of hiding and into the public eye; death is the other half of life and between life and death there is balance. This will be followed by Earth activity such as volcanos, drought, floods and extreme weather, war and radiation. As I am publishing this book there is a war in Ukraine and even now, not knowing how this war will end, it will bring change. Refugees will arrive needing to be cared for as brothers and sisters and the impetus is there to stop using fossil fuels.

The year of 2022 will be followed by a couple of years of adjustment to events, until life settles down again on a new pathway of light with hope for the future.

It is always important to use your own discernment when reading any channelled material to see whether it feels true to you.

Candace Caddick

May 2022

Introduction

This is a book about the ascension of the human soul. For many years on planet Earth individual souls have endeavoured to remember who they are and why they are here; what is the meaning of life and does God exist? Why can't people remember and why is it so hard to understand? So many theories and ideas have been put forward in an attempt to answer these questions, all in a genuine effort to make sense of the human experience of life and death. We who have written this book are angels, forming an Archangelic Collective. The Archangel Melchizadek is the primary author, assisted by other angels sharing our own particular vibration and expertise. We have watched the human race since your very beginnings and this book is offered with love to those of you who are ready to hear our teachings.

A long time ago we angels would walk among you and teach, often sitting by a river or in a clearing while you gathered around. Wandering tribes would listen to the universal truths of love that guide life on every planet. Our biggest impact was in the islands of Atlantis where, instead of passing through, you had settled and could return again and again to listen to our teachings (*Downfall of Atlantis*). Atlantis in its early eras was the pinnacle of your achievements in science and culture on Earth. In the end, Atlantis was destroyed from within. We were powerless to help as we do not coerce humans to act, only offering guidance for the highest good of all.

Today you have excelled in your spiritual growth, and bubbling under the surface of the consciousness of many people is the hunger to know why you are here. The search for answers extends beyond the traditional religions to the many spiritual teachers who echo our words of love. People are reaching out to glue themselves to the energy of love wherever they find it. It is a trend that is often unacknowledged by wider society, and it is a sign that people are beginning to remember that they are here on a mission - to know who they are and that they are souls that embody love.

It has been extremely difficult living on Earth for humanity, separated from love as they have been. In spite of that, humans are pulling themselves forward, step by step towards human ascension. This book was written for those who are searching for answers, to take you on a journey with explanations of where you are now, and how to get to the next level. It's important that the increasing flow of people these days who are reaching ascension continues to accelerate. This will allow humanity to achieve the critical mass necessary to collect every human on Earth together when it is time to step up as one soul. When the greater human soul ascends you will all ascend together, but some of you will have led the way. This is the challenge of these days and the events of Covid 19 and climate change will push you in that direction. This book covers the virus's impact on the human pathway, and where climate change is heading. It's all part of the plan to take humanity to ascension.

I am the Archangel Melchizadek and we are all very proud of those who daily try so hard to live by the universal laws that we taught you so long ago. "Treat everyone as you wish to be treated yourself." "Love thy neighbour as you love yourself." "Put the planet back the way you found it." These few rules will see humanity step over the threshold into the new Dawn of the Endless Day.

Archangel Melchizadek

I have written six previous books with the Archangels and they always want to write about something new, without repetition. Therefore, in the text I have put the names of the previous books near subjects that are explained in greater depth elsewhere, to assist any reader interested in further reading. In this book wherever I have referred to the Creator as He, it is solely to avoid the awkwardness of He/She. This series of books work well when read in order, but it is not a requirement for them to make sense; they are able to stand alone. This book, however, is best following *After We Die* as a continuation of the story that begins with Covid-19. All the books are still timely as the Archangels have written them to be relevant for years into the future.

Candace Caddick

Part One

The Gate Opens

1

How to Tell When it's Time to Die

WE ARE Archangels of light and we work together towards one goal, to bring the light of love into every heart on Earth. One of our methods is to engage a human being to write down our words for us. We have written seven books with this author about your life here on Earth: why you are here, what you expected of yourself for this lifetime and how to know when it's time for you to die and return home. It's that last question that is important at this time, the when and the how of dying. You know the why; your body gets older and less enjoyable to inhabit, or you came to Earth with a purpose and have completed it to your satisfaction. When either one of these two are in place you are free to leave and return again with a fresh, young body, and a new purpose. You have some flexibility with your end-of-life date and can choose the time when you wish to step through the door from this life into the afterlife. It's very much a decision to be based on joy and happiness. Whenever you emanate joy you continue to play a vital role on the planet.

You have been living with a plague called the Coronavirus, Covid-19, or SARS-Cov-2, and this has caused a wave of fear across much of the planet. And yet, it was a necessary experience for a species that had reached its end point. You are a soul of light, and are not prepared to see your living experience here on Earth end in failure with the destruction of your living planet and the loss of habitat suitable for human life. You cannot live in great numbers underwater or in temperatures over 50 ° C or Antarctic cold. Your billions would become thousands. Humanity has made some creative and brave choices and one of them was a contract with the virus for assistance.

This is not to say the virus was tasked with wiping out populations; its role was to increase the flow of energy around death and the entire process of dying. To help those who have spent years in painful bodies unnecessarily only because they have forgotten how to let go, or are afraid of what comes next; and those who have forgotten that they might return again one day, young and fresh, alive with a new purpose. To increase the flow around any subject reduces the amount of stagnant energy on the planet. We see flow and the free movement of energy as light, whereas stagnancy is dark energy, cold and solid. When you have a choice to change *anything* and take that choice, you are moving energy with your own decisions. If you live in stagnant energy you end up stuck in one place. Getting the energy moving around death will ultimately free many people to move on, so they can return one day to Earth for a new life.

People waiting to die are usually fearful. Who wouldn't fear the fires and eternal torments of hell? What a dark theory of cruelty and punishment that one is, feeding straight into the creation of fear and providing fuel for all beings of a dark nature. Others fear a nothingness after death, believing that when they die it is the ultimate end instead of the beginning of their next opportunity to learn about themselves. Remember that you are always alive and only sometimes you have a physical body. The Covid-19 virus will be with you until the energy around death begins to loosen and flow.

Not all who are afraid to die are the elderly. There are many throughout all the decades of life that are ready to die because they have completed their purpose in being on the planet. There are so many individual purposes, it is not possible to look at someone and guess correctly why they are here now. Even when you think it's obvious, don't guess. Look to your own lives and purposes instead, keep moving forward and don't let distractions bring you to a halt or a false turning. Especially now; all of you have roles to play and the need to fulfil your chosen purposes.

You have reached the end days for humanity, finding yourselves standing right at the edge of a cliff, while blindfolded. Those who have learned to remove their blindfolds are working to help the majority in an effort to bring everyone back from the edge. The virus helps create movement in more areas of life on Earth than death, and this movement will lessen fear. Instead of living on a planet paralysed by fear, blanketed in fear, and with minds clouded by fear, this is an opportunity to resume your search for joy. We hear the inner voices of the people of Earth, and they are crying out for help, for clarity and hope. This virus brings you hope, through bringing many, many changes.

2

The Earth's Axis Straightens

THERE was a time when an individual could incarnate with only a personal goal for their life, such as simply learning to say "no" after lifetimes of helplessness. Until around the year 2000, many who came to Earth were busy learning only one lesson in their life. Since then no one has incarnated with this type of personal goal. All babies born on the planet now are focused on completing humanity's overall plan, the one chosen by the greater human soul of which you are all a splinter. The new souls incarnating are fundamentally different. These new babies and children are not quite as separate from the whole, they are more connected and aware of other people on the edges of their consciousness. This is a huge change for humanity.

They have a greater sharing of the higher collective consciousness of mankind. The next generations will more easily feel one another's pain and happiness consistently, and have a clearer sense of the collective global lives of mankind. Compassion is unconditional love for others no matter who they are or what they do. There are many souls ready to jump onto Earth at the moment, all around the world. They are to be welcomed for the energy of love they carry. They will embody unconditional love and help turn back the tide of darkness. New thoughts and ideas will be measured against love, and if any new ideas do not enhance the level of love and light on the planet they will be discarded.

Young humans will also be in a hurry. There will be many quick learners, early to speak and walk. They will be driven by a shared goal of reversing not just the damage to the environment, but dismantling the systems that created the damage. Greed is not an aspect of love. Love is infinite, and every pebble on the planet will be cherished as they work together to repair the Earth.

Help has come from the many souls who have been working to anchor light on a planet of darkness. These older generations helped to create a future based on love, made possible by opening doorways to the light and allowing it to maintain a presence on Earth. They have reduced the dark blanket of energy covering the planet, constantly working to keep her healthy and alive by preventing her being smothered by the dark. The Earth herself is in a state of change.

The biggest single change that is coming in the near future will be the straightening of the axis of the North and South poles. The tilt in her axis came about as a result of the rampant instability of the humans living on her surface. There are so many of you, and your overall mental balance has long been askew. It has been this way as long as you can remember, and yet it was not always so. There are so many reasons for the way you often feel, as if you are just about coping with life. How many of you feel that everything in life is easy, all relationships are easy, your employment is a delight and your neighbours supportive and kind? Do you have time for everything, feel relaxed and are never anxious or stressed? This is not how most people feel now. They feel like they are just about hanging on by their fingernails and just one more thing will make them collapse. It's a mental health issue and most of you are the walking wounded, but showing no physical symptoms as you tell everyone you are "fine".

The Earth is sensitive to the energy of the people on her surface, and your lack of balance results in her lack of balance. Over she went, tilting on her axis, rolling around the sun at 23.5 degrees, and in the past almost tipping too far. Today she is held in a net of energy ropes running to her from her sister planets in the solar system, with other ropes coming from the stars. She is held and supported while slowly being pulled upright. If you fell over you would appreciate a helping hand and this is what is being held out to the Earth now. All such events take place at the perfect time for the highest good of all, and this is now the time for her to return to an upright position. This could happen in the next ten years or so. Every form of life on the planet will breathe a sigh of relief when the Earth has ceased to tilt and regained her balance.

Do you think humanity will be ready for such an event? The largest single event that can happen on a planet is for the poles to shift in this way. The latest generation of babies has been born to help prepare for this major happening, by holding a web of love across the planet. The strongest energy that can be brought to bear on any situation is unconditional love, and to create such a field will hold the people and planet with strength. It will happen at a time when there are fewer people on the planet, as the energy has already peaked on population numbers, preparing to head back down a bell curve. We are talking about the energy behind population growth, first the energy changes, then the physical reality. Much of your lower-lying land and islands will vanish, and wise preparation for this would be to move away from river deltas and low-lying areas like Florida. Humanity is being helped by the slow rise in sea levels, by slowly pushing people back and making them think about their futures. The Earth has cycles and you are coming out of one where a lot of your water was locked up in ice. It hasn't been very many hundreds of years since there were higher sea levels and it is routine for them to rise and fall. Your governments could plan for this rise in sea levels now if they wished. It will be a happy day when the poles straighten up, when living beings will have a balanced Earth under their feet again and an easier life living on a healthy planet.

The closest humanity has come to annihilation was when the poles began their slide towards the equator. Frantic, frenetic energy in humanity, senselessly scurrying and swarming like ants, where driving yourselves into mental breakdowns and alternate realities came with a price, the ability of the Earth to remain upright. She was swamped with your energy and her stability was shaken, resulting in tipping over on her side. There was a lot of attention from the other planets and stars focused on Earth at that time, because what happens here does not happen in a vacuum. The net of love was slung out from the Sun to the stars and other planets and her slide was arrested. She has often received planetary intensive care assistance ever since. The slow straightening of the Earth's axis over the past millennia has been laboriously gained, as little has changed on her surface. She will take the final steps to standing upright again much more rapidly.

We return to thoughts of death, as many of you may be thinking you don't care to live through a major event like the poles shifting. Not all of you need to, if it's not one of your planned purposes for this life, you are free to leave before this happens. Would you like to leave at the end of your life, or hang on in a nursing home waiting for the poles to shift? This is the ultimate gift of Covid-19, releasing the blockages around death so people can leave more easily when their lives are over, whether they are young or old. We don't mean that nursing homes should cease to exist, as some lives are planned to include an end-of-life experience in care, and some lives are planned to serve and look after these people. It is a good way to develop a strong sense of compassion and kindness and to live where you are cared for, if it is a part of your purpose. We are simply talking about the flow of energy around death and ease of dying. In a world of love there is space and acceptance for the elderly to live out their lives while being cared for.

3

Service Through Balance

IT IS because death is so misunderstood that the fear of dying infects and underpins the fears of scarcity and lack, loss of control, emptiness of lives and more. Death is the lack of life; and when alive these other fears are variations on this deepest fear. This is how brave each one of you is, to come to a planet and face these crippling fears while trying to remember who you are and why you are here. The good news is that you are remembering in ever greater numbers, and the human soul has made intrinsic changes that are helping to anchor light on the Earth. You once had to die before ascending, because it is so much easier to have the capacity to absorb all that extra information, memories of past learning, and higher vibrations into a brand new body than prepare a current body to receive a large download of your soul. Now the very work you do to ascend has prepared your physical bodies to hold all of this without dying first. You have begun to ascend within your lifetimes while continuing to live, and it is happening in ever greater numbers.

These new ascended masters are linked to every other ascended master, living or dead. They learned they are one with every form of life in the universe, and this comprehension links them together easily as a single soul. These masters bring a different perspective to their daily lives and teachings, drawing on the knowledge that is part of every ascended master. The ascended masters who are in spirit have always been a great reservoir of light for the human soul, and the accelerated creation of living ascended masters brings this light onto the Earth during their lifetimes. Once the new masters die they can choose whether or not to return to Earth for another life. Many have done this, motivated by love for humanity. At the time of writing we see over sixty living ascended masters on Earth, more than a doubling of the incarnate masters ten years ago, and these numbers are growing.

In the past there would be about twenty or so masters at a time who would volunteer to reincarnate on Earth and teach or simply start a change of direction. Some of them were permitted non-human bodies, like wolves or whales and dolphins. This was with the permission of those soul groups. Once one returned as an elemental. Another held the energy for the Sea King when he was trapped in other dimensions. (The Sea King looks like a kelpie.) When living in human bodies they have been involved with humanitarian work, teaching and frequently working behind the scenes. A very, very few came to be involved in religion, but each time their teachings were quickly corrupted within one or two generations. It's been a very long time since that experiment has been repeated, but you can imagine the thoughts behind one of those lifetimes. "I'll tell them to love everyone, and to love their neighbours as much as they love themselves. It's really very simple to learn who you are that way." They weren't successful.

Now you might identify these masters and mistresses by catching a glimpse of their teachings on the internet or in a book, maybe on TV or radio. They are speaking to *you*. These messages are not for everyone, for not everyone is ready at the moment to love their neighbour as themselves. They are looking away from that message. But many people are searching for knowledge and finding it in a voice that speaks to them in a way they can understand. That is why we speak through many different messengers. It's not just the languages they speak, but also when they speak in your own language what are their word choices? If they make their message clear to you then continue to study what that person is bringing to you.

An important part of your search for knowledge is daily meditation. We are able to speak directly to you when you are in an altered state and your brain has relaxed. Meditation brings you closest to our vibration, and in addition you will be spending time with yourself, the real self that exists outside your body, your immortal soul. Spending time with your soul is the smartest way to access the knowledge held there from many lifetimes' worth of experiences and learning. For those of you who can hear us, we can offer guidance most easily when you are meditating. We would see everyone meditate every day for their own mental health and spiritual growth as it allows your brain to rest. Meditation can smooth out the mental wrinkles which lead to clarity and positive thinking. Whether silent or guided by someone else, meditation will help you.

We see you as you go about your daily lives, we see you as small moving beings of light or dark or shades of grey. We see the vibrations you emit of fear or love, and we see the calm and collected energy in capable people who are in control of their lives and emotions. These people are enjoying their lives more than many others and in most cases they are the ones who spend time in meditation. Meditate for yourself and encourage others to do so, and promote meditation for school children and teachers. You have this tool to change your lives, and by extension the world you live in as you unblock your ability to hold more light in your bodies each day.

We also wish to point out that holding more light and more balance is a way to help the planet. Never has it been more important to be grounded and balanced, pursuing your own enlightenment and understanding, and discover why your past made you the person you are today. Balanced energy is catching and it can spread through communities and out into wider society. Like an inverted triangle, the balanced person on the bottom easily supports an ever growing number of balanced people. Just like love, balance is infinite, there is always enough balance to go around. If the only job you did in this life was to be balanced and stabilize a community you would have done mighty work. Especially in these unstable times you will stabilize others by simply letting your energy exist in their world. Perhaps you sometimes feel you calm other people down in conversations. That is your own balance speaking through you. Work at this through meditation, and if you practice Reiki or another form of self-healing daily that will also help to maintain balance.

4

The War on Balance

PEOPLE today are pulled out of balance by those who wish to manipulate others for their own purposes, usually power and money. The rise of social media has made this very easy with lies spreading faster than they can be proved wrong. It takes effort to speak the truth and check your facts before you speak or write, far more effort than it takes to spin a lie to get what you want. For this reason you need to practice distancing yourselves from all posts to begin with, saying to yourselves "This may not be true. I don't know enough to know if it is true or false so I will move on and ignore it." Not many of you choose to deliberately lie to people when you are face to face or spread hatred, but you carelessly share false posts and spread lies on or from the internet.

Distancing yourself from all posts will give your emotions a rest and allow you to feel like your true self again. This then allows you to use your own level of vibration to assess the way some posts make you feel. If it does not feel right to you it could be false. The important thing is that if you have any doubts you never share it further. In fact, the less time you spend on all the social media sites, the better it is for you. We can see the beneficial side to these sites, allowing you to stay in contact with friends and relatives. The posts we are referring to are either political or commercial, designed to influence your behaviour. You are dipping your toes into a stream of toxic sludge, how deep do you want to go and how long will you risk staying in there? You need to exercise control to escape unharmed.

The emotional manipulation does not stop with the internet as this is also the role some newspapers, TV and radio stations were created for by their owners. Lies create fear and by pushing out lies about possible threats the fear is entrenched, creating changes in behaviour. It is almost impossible to find out the truth as a common citizen without access to the information about what is really happening. It's so important to stop and distance yourself from all sources of information designed to *raise your emotions*. Give it space to settle and wait for more information to come forward, don't talk about it or spread it further. It's your own balance and well-being we are trying to protect here. Your being balanced in the world is one of the most important jobs you have.

On the internet you can find people who are very excited about the latest outrage by their political opponents. In this state of mind they are uselessly causing a large energetic imbalance that you will have to counteract with the way you live your own life. The Earth needs balance; everybody needs balance more than anything else at the moment. When you step back from false or incendiary posts you not only don't add fuel to the fire, but you are calming them down by your own actions. If you get angry at a politician, let it go for no other reason than it is not for the highest good of all. You add fuel to the fire with your anger.

Does that mean you can never take any action no matter how you feel about what's happening in the wider world? There are a lot of positive actions you can take, from running for office yourself to supporting someone you admire. Outside of politics there are many fields looking for honest and engaged workers. The energy of anger can be used to create positive change, although anger is an energy source that can twist in your hands and hurt you. Working with positive sources of energy such as compassion is preferable. The positive action has to come from somewhere to balance the darkness of negativity and you will benefit personally if it comes from or through you.

Right now balance is needed to repair the natural cycles of rain and sun for growing crops, moderate natural Earth catastrophes, calm the climate and slow the melting of ice. Everyone who steps back from anger and lies will be adding balance by not engaging. There is a war on for continued life on the planet taking place right now, with everyone on a losing side unless you can re-establish balance.

5

Conspiracy Theories

A NOTHER way to avoid instability is to keep at arm's length from today's volatile current events. We do actually want you to know what is happening in your world as ignorance is itself unstable, otherwise you have nothing to grab hold of or stand on. You are then easy prey for those who wish to sell a false reality. However, we don't recommend continually checking the news on your devices and worrying, once a day is often enough. It allows you to follow the human environment you live in without succumbing to an overload of anxiety. You live in the end times of rapid change and if you decide to opt-out and choose ignorance then you are not fitting yourself to play the role you came to play. If you are not participating in life on Earth, then do you need to be here anymore? Some people are physically immobile but holding energy and balance for all of you, including many of the elderly. What is your potential, and are you able to rise to it?

Not all sources of information are to be trusted. How do you know who to trust and who to avoid? It is common for all governments to lie to their people most of their time. We can see it so clearly ourselves, but we see it only as a wide range of shades of grey. Therefore you must train your senses to be more like the angels, whether it is sight, sound, or feelings. We look for the light that is an aspect of truth, and see how much of it is present in any story. A story that is mostly true reports what happened, leaving out many smaller details to fit into the time or space available. A story that is spun with lies you can feel with all your senses, there is no point trying to isolate which senses, but somewhere in your body. For instance you may feel revulsion, or you can't listen to it, or something about it is making you feel like vomiting. These are common feelings. Lies will make you feel unstable, activate your suspicions, cause you to fear and worry. Your reaction as a soul of light to lies is predictable.

Why are so many people (including light workers) being swayed today by modern conspiracy theories? There have always been conspiracy theories that have grown up around the unknowable. Today you are not in a position to really know any number of things that happened in the past. You have a choice: do you anchor yourself into these past events and sway and be enthralled with conflicting theories, or do you shrug your shoulders, say "I will never know what happened there" and move into your own future balanced and stable. It's hard to admit you will never know all the answers about events that happen in your lifetime, but theories like these have been promulgated for hundreds of years. Conspiracy theories are destabilizing, and have been concocted many, many times in the past because the originators desire the chaos and the darkness to help them get what they want.

The present conspiracy theories are almost one hundred percent false. How are you going to find that one percent of truth that is folded into them? They have grown and been amplified deliberately to cause instability, with darkness creating more darkness. If you choose to engage with them you are putting yourself at risk. We see you as your energy changes from curious onlooker to eager, excited participant, recruiting others so these theories can spread farther and faster. Yet these new theories are often the same as the old ones; they are distractions to living your own life in light and moving forward in a balanced and stable way while holding the light up for all to see. What happens when there is light? It's easier to see what is true and what is false. Avoid them all, do not engage.

Some of you may be thinking about your own involvement in spreading conspiracy theories and wondering now what is and is not really true. Did you invest your own energy and reputation in promoting something that is lies? What stops you admitting this to yourself? Usually it is personal ego. If you can admit to yourself that you have no evidence of actions taken that are in line with what you have read and believe, then that is the place to start in self examination. If your sole source of information is single author web-based material or pod cast, then contrast it to what you see and hear with your own eyes. We remind you that it is "by their actions you will know them." Look at news films and photos that are current, not photo-shopped days later.

A noticeable side-effect of reading and spreading conspiracy theories is that the energy fields over the head and heart vanish leaving a person with an incomplete energy field. Why does this matter? There is no longer any energy for the brain, ears or eyes to assess the world around them, and no heart energy for compassion. In our point of view these people have made a strange choice to become thus impaired. As time passes you can see on current event programs the energy fields of the most active spreaders of lies dropping down past their waists and knees. Watch the films taken at the attack on the US Capitol and see if you can spot any protestor whose energy field goes above his head. Without energy there is no life.

Main stream media has been guilty of omissions in reporting news over the years, many times hiding and slanting the truth to protect private interests. But there still exists a public service element on the genuine news channels and newspapers, otherwise they would be like the news in Kyrgyzstan, which only offers a continuous stream of stories praising its President. Stories must have more than one source before they are printed or aired. That means you don't interview two people from one office telling the same story, you find more witnesses from separate spheres. This is not perfect and some news organisations are better than others, but it carries more truth and light than single author web-based material. We rate seeing the news happen with your own eyes as the best source, followed by hearing about it on TV or radio. You need to see and hear some people to feel that visceral reaction in your body. You need to know who owns your newspapers and TV and radio as they vary so greatly and some of them are very untruthful. How does your newspaper make you feel when you've finished with it? Have your emotions been manipulated into anger, fear and outrage? You're being used. We rank the major city broadsheet newspapers and local papers as being about eighty percent true. That's a big difference from the one percent of online theories.

We angels are supporting the main stream media because we promote stability and balance to help people and the Earth. For all their flaws, they still report information so that people can see what is happening and draw their own conclusions. The web-based conspiracy theories are intended to promote instability and darkness, lies being the prime form of darkness that leads to everything else. (See the section written by the Archangel of Darkness in *Planet Earth Today*.) They are not accidentally having this effect, they are designed to hook people in and keep them coming back for more, destabilizing their readers so they are easier to manipulate. We see this, and it makes us sad. We are taking the opportunity this book provides to give our views on this subject.

6

The QAnon Conspiracy

WHAT IS in the latest crop of conspiracy theories that differentiates them from those in the past? One of the cruellest is the QAnon conspiracy, accusing known Democrat politicians of international child trafficking, abusing children, using them in Satanic rituals, drinking children's blood among other things, familiar lies taken from the past and now attached to modern politicians. There is nothing new in its make-up. It is a recycling of the century's old Protocols of Zion anti-Semitic slanders - horrific and sickening stories that are false whether said about Jews or modern day Democrats. There are many details recycled from so many other past conspiracy theories that we are pretty sure nothing has been omitted if it could have been squeezed in. And yet, these have taken hold of people and ensnared them and they are believed whole-heartedly. The internet has helped them to spread rapidly.

The internet can be seen as a vast network of tubes, what one person inserts at one end you receive in your home at your end. How many of you are able to see the energy that comes through your screens and into your homes from your computers or televisions? Some websites are set up as traps, and you are not going to know which ones they are until you click on them. If you ever feel uneasy about a webpage, get straight off it. When opening a home page their energy comes through into your office, kitchen, or wherever you are reading. The wrong kind of website spews black energy into your home and covers you with something like tar. It's very hard to remove even if you realise you are coated with it in the first place. We see many of you sitting in your homes in rooms filled with filthy black energy and we can hardly see you, covered in that same tar-like substance. Sad to say, many new age and healing sites have been set up as traps and you need to be very aware and so careful when you are browsing the web. If it doesn't feel right, it is wrong.

The multitude of conspiracy websites are the same, and once you have been covered in a thick coating of black tarry energy you carry the same energy as the sites. You have become ensnared. You have no defences at all when your energy has been submerged in that of the sites. Many people no longer seem to have any ability to find and use their native discernment. There are the added ego problems of excitement when you think you know what's really happening and others do not. Very few readers are still whole enough mentally to admit to themselves that their energy has changed and walk away unscathed. Few of those mislead by QAnon will have the strength to break away.

This is a problem that cannot be underestimated for the Earth as a destabilizing force on an already unstable planet. It requires the rest of you to practice being balanced to counteract these misled victims, to help yourself and the planet. If you feel tarnished by these sites and wish to rid yourself of this energy then the best way is to go outside, ground and be aware of nature and your vital role in helping the planet, while wishing to be free of any negative energy. Ask angels to help with clearing you off. Trees will help to clear you if you ask for their help. When you are outside you are not sitting in a black energy cave inside your home. Practice grounding yourself frequently in the Earth's energy, practice self-healing modalities like Reiki and moving meditations like yoga or tai chi, and the most effective of all; spend your time outside in nature.

QAnon had its origins in money, with those who can never have enough money or power and who routinely scattershot schemes and actions to see which ones take hold and work to their benefit. These are the same "powers that be" supporting conspiracy sites promoting QAnon that pretend they are opposing themselves in their conspiracy writings. QAnon is the creation of an inner circle of the wealthy establishment. It distracts you from genuine dialogue and reform to the status quo by creating new targets to attack. Money buys more money.

When you are free of darkness you will be able to realise by using your own discernment that the instigators of a big money conspiracy like QAnon aimed at destroying Democrats is the Republican Party and its backers, to help them win elections and stay in power. If you have been having trouble making this extremely simple connection of who is benefiting from these slanders, then please ask us for our help in clearing you off. We have one group of angels who are experts at removing this type of energy, and if you ask them to help they will clean your body and energy fields and your home environment. Candace calls them the "spring cleaning angels" and they will answer to that name. Then ask them to transform all the darkness they remove into light to improve the dark/light balance on the planet.

You who are reading this book learned in the past about love, how it feels and how it forms your behaviour. When you stand in a place of love you do not malign or hurt another, you use your discernment to act with integrity and come from a place of truth. Integrity reveals deception and is not dishonest. When we stand in our truth we are not offering our opinion, it is not based on antiquated belief systems, nor based on popular theories, but on how the universe truly works. If your truth hurts another it cannot be the truth. Humanity is learning this lesson at this time but it must be learned individually and all must learn to recognise and speak from their place of love and light and anything else is deception. If your words are not coming from a place of love, they are not the truth nor are you acting for the highest good of all. Lies don't lead to a higher level of ascension and your thoughts and words matter. Love = joy = truth = light.

Conspiracy theories are created to divert your attention away from something else, so that other actions can pass unchallenged. They can be very efficient at doing this, by offering excitement and exclusivity, usually taking their adherents willingly further down a path their feet were already walking on, while justifying their past thoughts and beliefs. It's an addiction that is very hard to break once a person has immersed themselves in conspiracies. For this reason we seriously advise all readers to shun them entirely. There is a road of light on Earth, growing stronger every day, keep your feet on that road instead.

7

Beginning the Process of Change

YOU ARE living in a time of great change, brought about by your failure to make the small changes when they were needed in the past. Molehills have become mountains, and are harder to level out easily again. If your goal is to rescue the planet and help humanity ascend then these two tasks are intertwined. The planet is degraded by human activity, saving the planet by changing the way humans treat her will show that the final lesson has been learned and you are approaching your own ascension. This activity of regenerating the planet is now the main highway to soul ascension. Whether this is one person working alone or with many, these steps are all heading straight to the light.

There are many ways to help regenerate a planet. We angels sponsor more than one healing group, such as Candace and Grainne Warner's online Earth Magic Healing Circle. Its role is to create blueprints and pathways for future planetary change and is always open to newcomers. They are having an affect already by planting energy seeds in the world, ready to be picked up and used by others. Additional Earth healing groups are targeted at local or worldwide problems and people join them because they are suited to their particular ways of working. Many people incarnated to help the planet and are interested in joining an Earth healing group. Other people have the knowledge and skills to work directly with the land thereby contributing in many different ways, while some are skilled in committee work or in organising small or large projects. All ways of working that help the Earth are important and necessary for progress.

One change everyone can make is the way they live in their homes by doing their utmost to reduce their carbon footprints, use less plastic and fewer powerful cleaning chemicals. By following all the positive living advice written by the experts who have studied the harmful effects of your lifestyles you will make a difference. You can do this, one step at a time. Every time you buy something new do it thoughtfully and don't repeat past mistakes. Many of you don't think about what you buy until after you've brought it home. This needs to become an urgent, top priority for all of you. You will be living in a new way from now on. The old way is not sustainable, please don't add anything else to the Earth's problems.

How many years do you have remaining to turn this around? It is 2021 when we are writing this book, and if you can't make serious progress by 2024 then you could well run out of time living in the manner you are accustomed to. Climate change and Earth degradation will force you onto a rough and uncertain path. If you think it's hard to give up plastic bottles today, in a few years time these problems will have snowballed and people's lives will have to change dramatically. Your home may survive intact, but the number of climate refugees arriving may be overwhelming, while your own climate shifts out of control. Contrast this with improving the climate so that people can remain in their homes, perhaps on their farms, and not be refugees. The wild climate changes are manmade and the softer cyclical alterations that are always present are never as destructive or extreme. Slower natural cycles give people more time to adjust and take the changes into account. Please take the climate crisis seriously.

We ask each of you therefore to 1) find your own purpose and help the Earth in the way that fits you best, 2) shop like your every purchase is vitally important. Consider what it is, what it is made from, how many air miles, its carbon footprint, whether you need it, is it recyclable, etc. There are up-to-date tables with much of this product information available online. You will be leading the way by setting an example, and refusing to be part of the problem to the best of your ability. We are beings of energy and we see how the energy changes when you change your habits. You establish a new vibration right where you live and it spreads to others. This is how change happens: the actions you take set up a new energy field and the actions you neglect change nothing. It's not enough to hope someone else will make the changes necessary, such as governments. When you hear a phrase like "there is a new breeze blowing" through any stagnant situation, such as government inaction, that breeze begins with the actions individuals take. Take the actions you are able to take and encourage others to do so likewise.

By loving and cherishing the Earth's beauty you live at a higher vibration closer to her own. This makes a difference as she exists at a vibration of love herself, while paying host to billions of people who are holding a lower vibration. We're not saying there aren't exceptions, but they are very few overall. By spending as much of your day as possible with your hearts holding love you will help change everything in human society and on the Earth. When humans learn to hold love to the same degree as the planet, she won't have to work so hard to counteract the lower energy. This drag on her own energy is similar to yours when you are cold and your body has to work harder to keep warm enough. She has to work hard to stay balanced. Love is the vibration that will help her balance while the opposite pulls her over.

The opposing energy can be expressed as anger, greed and war. In the war-torn countries around the world, like the Sudan, physical devastation of the environment beats anything the climate has done. War has degraded pasture land by turning it into desert, and forced the people to leave their homes. Many of today's former farm lands can no longer grow crops without first regenerating the land. We often mention farmers in our books because you need food to live on this planet, and you are very careless in preserving your growing areas. Loving everyone enough to value all lives would change the way you treat everything in existence. You would want everyone to have a happy and safe life and fight to end wars over land and profits. Soldiers rarely know the real reasons they are fighting, but it is usually to enrich someone far removed from them. Using boys to fight and die for money is despicable, but it has been the way of humanity for thousands of years. It's a burden of darkness that stains your human soul.

8

The Energy of Manifestation

THERE were times in the past when farming was
productive and people were fed, but all the workers
were slaves and unhappy in their lives. It's not enough to be
fed, each person has to be treated as an equal, as only then do
you regain the potential and the strength you were born with.
We have written in *Planet Earth Today* to look into everyone's
eyes and see yourself looking back. You are splinters of one
great soul, so how can you all fail to be the same? Very, very
few see others as human beings with exactly the same rights
for a happy life that they claim for themselves. They fail to
see their mutual humanity and having failed at this important
understanding have diminished themselves. Instead of
belonging to the strong family of humanity, they go it alone
by feeling superior to others. They exist without an essential
part of their understanding; they are not whole people but
are weakened by this lack. You know these people are among
you and they are exactly the ones who are prepared to hurt
others and cause imbalance through their lack of love. They
take hurtful actions and these ripple out through families and
friends. Pity them, pity the burden they have created for their
souls at a time when they are at their weakest to carry the
burden. Do your best to love them and so not lose a portion
of your own soul to hate and thereby weakening your own
strength. Pity them, but do not follow their lead.

You have a number of these people on your planet right now,

and how are you going to balance and be happy when they use their money to buy positions of leadership? They make it harder for you, but the answer is still love and compassion for all to bring change to any situation on Earth. Any time you think you have run up against an immovable problem, use love to soften it and change the energy around it. The basic starting point is to look at it and say, "I don't know everything, but I would like this problem resolved <u>for the highest good of all</u>." Then choose what method you will use to send light to any problem or difficulty. Many people pray, but ask only for their own desires. These prayers are devoid of love when praying to twist a result to the one that they want regardless of anyone else. These prayers remain close by, in the energy fields of the supplicant, rarely going any further and this person will have to answer their own prayers. Reiki practitioners can send Reiki for the highest good of all, as can all the other healers working with the same energy but calling it by another name. Healers who work with light regularly will have been changed by their continued contact with it, the light being another name for love. Prayer can also be a tremendous force for good, although we see a lesser understanding in many people of how to pray effectively.

What about those times when you want to create something good for yourself? As long as you surrender to your request of it being for the highest good of all, go ahead and ask - with purpose and joy. Look up and out and let your desire flow freely out from you heart to where it can be heard and answered. We want you to do this, to focus your attention on yourself sometimes and find out what you really want to have or do. If you never do this how will you get to know yourself? Often a change in direction is desperately needed, and it is far better to properly consider what change may best fit with your purpose. Then you will know how to frame a request and send it out to the universe, God, or your higher self. You will get your best results after having spent time in serious contemplation. Your lives are each so different and you have different ways of accessing the energy around you to manifest your desires in your lives. This is just one way to try. You are not flotsam to be pushed here and there by the events of your lives. You are responsible souls, the best there are or have been, and you have the ability to shape a life along the lines you initially planned for yourself, and never simply drift.

The days are gone now when people were free to incarnate to "just have a go" at life, with little serious idea of what they wanted to achieve from their time on Earth. You still have some of these people alive now on Earth, although not as many as there once were, and there have not been any more incarnated for twenty-five years or so. As the Earth was stripped of animals and life these carefree souls no longer suited the greater human soul's requirements. Instead, the most recent souls to be born on your planet are so determined to help the human soul succeed that they have deep and multilayered purposes. They are advanced and mature souls who can handle the hard work and the challenge, and lead multi-tasking lives. They still have joy and joyful times in their lives, but successfully following their soul's plan really makes them happy. Balancing the Earth and reclaiming areas that have suffered degradation is why they are here, and they are satisfied and fulfilled by working on her behalf. If you hear "young people don't know how to have fun anymore", they are different from their elders. They are content with

31

what they are accomplishing for the planet with hard work and focus.

The children born after 2012 look at the future of their planet and are afraid for her. They are too young to fully step into their roles, and they need older people to buy them time until they are in possession of their full strength of body and mind. They will be ready at a young age to begin their labours, but at the time of writing the eldest of them are barely ten years old. This is not their job for now, but if you all play your parts you will move heaven and Earth to give them a fair chance of healing the Earth. Your role is to create an environment that is moving away from greedy destruction towards healing, to turn a sharp corner and bring about a dramatic change in direction. This is a job you will start for others to finish, but if you do not start there will not be enough time to finish. What are you as an individual able to do, and what can you do when you join with others? Do what you can alone, and look for others who will work with you. Deep inside all of you is love of the Earth and a willingness to work at setting things right to inspire and fulfil you. You did not come here to destroy the Earth, you came to rescue her.

9
The Opening of the Stellar Gateway

YOU HAVE your young people in place on the planet now, with more being born every day. Humans are here to help the Earth pass through a stellar gateway that is approaching in the not-too-distant future. It will be a process of guiding her, adjusting her trajectory, holding her steady and keeping her straight on her path. The closest you have to this on Earth is a horse and carriage where the coachman guides the team down a road and through an archway. You are not at this time ready to help guide her. She is not stable in herself, there is too much unbalanced energy and she is shaky. The uncertainties today lead to polarised, unstable energy. All of you need to prioritise time for yourselves to balance and meditate, connecting to a higher plane that is peaceful and supportive. All your lives will change for the better with more meditation.

The solar system is waiting for humans to remember who they are and take their place as part of the community of life on Earth. The stellar gateway will open a direct passage from this reality to a new reality of existence. Earth will once again be balanced, signalling the remaining planets in the solar system to follow her through the gate. The other planets have been ready to go for quite a while now, but because they love the Earth, their sister, they have stayed and held her and supported her through hard times. The stellar gateway will open and dissolve the barrier between realities allowing all these planets to pass through, almost sucked through, behind the Earth. Last of all will be the Sun who has worked to bring them to ascension, in the same way as the planets were working with other soul groups.

On the other side of the gateway are the planets and stars who have gone before. Some of these planets are vast and old beyond imagining. Planets four times the size of Jupiter, ancient with cracked surfaces that have been waiting for the gate to open again and a new wave of planets to come through. These ancient planets have been helping to hold the balance in the universe between the seen and the unseen. They will have a big welcome for this solar system's arrival in the higher dimensions having waited a long time to begin the next phase of their own existence. If you think if your world is colourful now, the new existence will be that much more richly coloured and filled with life. You would not exchange the new Earth for the old if you could.

This is not the end, it is a new beginning. It's not heaven, but it will be beautiful and healthy and the souls on the planets will have worked through many difficult challenges to bring their worlds to this gateway. The beings on these planets will have ascended and have moved up a level to continue their learning about life in these new circumstances. Earth will be different, as she had to be cleaned and repaired before she was ready to go and join the others, and the people present will have worked hard to do this. A regenerated, healthy Earth will host the next round of inhabitants until the final big step at the end of the Universe.

Part Two

Finishing on a High

10

Creating the Future

W E'VE previously written that humanity is very close to ending it's time on Earth in an ascended state. The answer to "when will it happen?" swings forward a little, back a little, jumps from one timeline to another, then jumps back again. Some people have the ability to lead humanity toward creating a healthy Earth, while others look only at money and disregard the cost of their activities to the planet. You are close to running out of time for ascension if you can't find the inner willpower to change the way you live. More and more people wish to give up those things in modern life that lead to planetary death and the end of the human race. They do not value money over a living planet, but there are a host of obstacles in their way.

Incredibly, and in the face of overwhelming scientific evidence, only a few tiny countries like Costa Rica are prepared to radically change their policies to protect the planet. In other countries the governments find any excuse to approve another coal mine or fossil fuel project, no matter what its environmental impact is calculated to be. This is in spite of signed treaties and stated policies to protect the planet. Governments do this because they don't believe the planet is as important as being re-elected, so they provide jobs in coal and oil instead of developing clean energy and providing alternative employment. Usually this is because fossil fuel companies generously support political parties and make it worthwhile for politicians to subsidize them in return and commission new pipelines, oil fields, etc. One month after the end of hosting the COP26 climate conference in Glasgow the Prime Minister, Boris Johnson, approved new licenses to drill in the North Sea for oil to preserve jobs.

If you want these political parties to stop these harmful policies, now, today, before it gets any worse, you are going to have to join together in protest and not just leave it up to a few activists. Some people have been disproportionately carrying the load and need the active support of everyone else now. How are you going to help? Writing letters, donate money, make phone calls, organise petitions, join a protest march? It is time to step up your game here and take part. Why? Because you came here to do exactly that! You came to save the planet with your actions. You were without a body in timelessness and said, "Let me to the front of the line for births, I want to get down to Earth and help." You're here now, and inside there is still this strong desire to help. Everyone can find their best way to do this, and you won't all be helping in the same way as you are so different from each other. Find your own way and spend enough time actively doing it to make a difference and one day, having done your best, you will feel happy and fulfilled. The flip side to not doing your best is to be back one day on the other side of the veil between life and death, and realise with horror you failed in your only important job and wasted your chance. It happens, we've seen souls choose to come to Earth again as a baby and repeat the task, but today you are nearly out of time in the physical world. Get busy helping now as a competent adult.

There is justified frustration at the slowness of large corporations to remove single use plastic from their products in grocery stores and elsewhere. You can boycott these goods, or in many cases remove the packaging and leave it behind in the supermarket. This is not a terrible or harmful thing to do, leaving plastic behind. Endlessly creating and forcing you to buy single use plastic is terrible and harmful to your planet. Some of the better firms stopped using it and all manufacturers will need to change their ways until the only plastic in use is purposeful and long-term. When you develop new materials you can replace any of the reusable plastic items. Today we see aisles in supermarkets towering with goods in plastic wrap or plastic single-use bottles. If your local grocery store looks like this, then think how many of these there are in the world and how your supermarket is only one of them. Go ahead, be the first person you know to leave your plastic behind in the store. This tactic was used successfully in Germany by the Green Party to reduce packaging, along with offering payment for returning empty plastic bottles for recycling in supermarkets.

The world changes, yet some things are very stubborn to change such as fossil fuel powered cars. If you buy an electric car you will still need a power station to create the electricity for it to run on, and that station is using resources while producing pollution, although electric cars are an overall environmental improvement on diesel cars. Are you the person who will devise a new method of clean transport? So much has to change to get people out of their cars and airplanes, more than just changing transport there needs to be fewer journeys, fewer miles flown or driven, and more places to go within walking distance.

11

Remembering How to Die

DEATH has always been present on Earth, but has accumulated too much baggage over the millennia from religions, societies, and most of all from being divorced from the natural world. There is pain and sadness at the separation from loved ones. The Covid -19 virus has taken on the huge job of relaxing attitudes to death, until the fear subsides and the passing is once again easy. This is not a short term plan, and you are just at the beginning. There are conversations taking place around death now where a greater proportion of the adult population is giving serious thought to how they want to end their days. In the end they will remember how to die.

Alone of the residents on Earth, humanity forgot how to die and leave the planet. We have watched as many people who wished to end their lives created a fatal disease, regarding it as a sure way to leave the planet. The wall between the conscious and subconscious minds in these people won't allow themselves to know that this is the path they have chosen. When you know you have completed what you came to do on Earth you are free to leave, painlessly. Then you can come back with a new purpose and a fresh young body.

Perhaps this is hard for you to understand at the moment. What if you think of it as living without fear of dying? Not recklessly, but with a calm acceptance that the afterlife is not something to fear. Is it death and loss of your loved ones that makes you afraid, or is it the afterlife? Covid-19 is training you to lose your loved ones, in the same way as when pets die they teach children how to live with death. Humanity is relatively behind in this training, but it will help later to have lived through this pain. Acceptance of the deaths of others eases the acceptance of your own death. With this change in acceptance there will be incremental increases around the ease of dying, not by looking for additional deaths, but that the deaths that are taking place are easier for all: deaths free of lingering pain or sadness. Death comes for everyone at the end of their lives and it can be as easy as falling asleep in your bed at home.

Covid-19 is a sentient soul, invited to this planet in virus form by humanity to help people learn to die. For this reason it will be with you for a little while longer, mutating and jumping from country to country, while returning in waves. Those who die from the virus will almost exclusively be those who are at the end of their lives already. You may have a preconception that the end of life comes in old age, but remember the end of life is when you are finished and your purpose is completed. You won't necessarily remember what your chosen purpose was, but most of you have happily stumbled onto it during this life. At some point you will be finished and then you are free to go, or stay on Earth and spend more time with your families for a little while. If you are healthy you may wish to stay, and if you are unwell or unhappy you are free to leave. Covid is trying to teach you to exit with ease. It is ok to die and you do not have to stay after you are ready to leave.

Let's say you are in hospital and you feel that enough is enough and you are ready to die. How do you do that? In most cases following these steps will help ease your passing.

1) Ask to see your families and let them say goodbye and release you to die.

2) When these ties are released, form the intention to leave either while they are there or when they are gone, it is up to you.

3) You can ask angels to help escort you from life so you don't have to go alone.

4) Don't panic, let go of everything and breathe out, relax and bit by bit and allow yourself to become unstuck. Take a nap and let it happen while you are asleep after saying to yourself "it is my wish and intention to go while asleep" and trust that your word is enough to make it happen. You're in charge here.

5) Repeat if necessary and look at what you may be holding on to, such as fears about dying and the afterlife. Reread our earlier book, *After We Die*, to be reminded of the true afterlife that awaits you.

We offer the suggestions above with love. The love in the outer universe is waiting for all of you who have been shut on Earth for so long with so little love in your lives. You may feel that we are wrong, that you have plenty of love in your life. We are talking about the love of all of Creation as opposed to the love of a few family members. That much love would be overwhelming if you were not used to it, but you are. Every time you have ended one life and are waiting for the next you bask in this love as it fills every corner of your being. You fill yourselves up and remember that this is how it always is when you are Home, before you make another sojourn on Earth. This is why we do not envy you or wish we could trade places with you, as your lives on Earth contain such meagre amounts of love. And yet, some of you have learned about yourselves as a small part of the Creator Who Loves Us All to the point where you can see your relationship to the entire universe and the life it contains. You have used loneliness and separation as tools to push you into this understanding. We would rather hit our heads against a brick wall for a thousand years than do what you have done here, living without love. We honour your courage with all our hearts.

Angels help humans because of the respect we have for the difficult task you chose. Because everything in the universe is one and we are all tiny particles of the same Creator, the impossibly hard lessons humanity has experienced here are learned on behalf of every form of life in the universe. This love and respect is why the Earth - with its animals, insects, rocks and bacteria - continues to wait for you to ascend. Just as all humans go together, all forms of life will one day go together to return to the Creator. Every being on Earth will wait for you, if possible, because of the heart-breakingly difficult game you have played on Earth. When you look around at people who are very different from you and whom you may not like, remember that they are you and have also struggled through this insanely hard life to reach an understanding of who they are and why they are here. Your struggles in the absence of love have matched their struggles. Whatever else has made up your lives, you all share this most difficult aspect of life on Earth.

12

Crises Large and Small

FOLLOWING the Covid-19 pandemic there will be more equanimity surrounding death among those remaining on the planet. Death will have touched many families and the expectations about how lives can end will have changed for good. At the moment too many people see life as finishing in a nursing home, possibly with mental degeneration or physical weakness, lonely for family visits, bored, and then perhaps a painful death so they can exit the planet. A quicker death is possible starting with cutting out the painful part. No one needs to anticipate dying in pain. This adjustment will free all lives to be lived without the fear of a painful death. As we said, it is the fear of death that is your biggest human fear, wrapping your planet in a dismal shroud. We just want you to live free and happy.

While you have been transfixed by the virus your climate crisis has sped up through various actions, or lack of actions, taken by the world governments. This is the biggest threat to life worldwide through turning the Earth into a planet where you can no longer find your own environmental niche to live in. We can hardly bear to watch this happening any longer, but we are here to help you in any way we can when you ask us for help. There is actually much that can be done right now. There is, however, a caveat: some of the "miracle" repairs will not be done until the continuing damage stops. The oceans won't be brought back to life while nothing has changed in over-fishing or polluting them, and so on. First you need to stop and then there are a variety of beings, from elementals, aliens, some humans, angels and others ready to step in with transformative help. At this point in time, you haven't yet begun to pull back on your actions and therefore we can't help you. Do everything in your power to change the direction people are heading with the climate crisis. There isn't much time left. It will form a second global crisis along with the virus.

These types of large crises tends to initiate smaller ones like pebbles rolling down a hill in an avalanche. Where do you concentrate your own energy in these circumstances? We've talked about living in the most planet-friendly way you can, and supporting all those who work for the planet differently from you. Pester your governments and corporations to do their jobs better. But what are these other, unknown crises? They are likely to be regional wars, regional tragedies of famine, or natural disasters like Earth quakes, volcanoes, etc. Planetary degradation will lead to scarce resources. This is obvious and we have to wonder why this isn't daily headline news, or at the top of every government's agenda? All of these smaller scenarios caused by the climate crisis will need preventative actions by those who care. We know you care and we are encouraging you to act. Find your way of contributing to make things right again.

We write about the Earth, this planet we love, in our books. When you are able to quiet your minds and look around you, you will see that all humans love the planet. This "looking around" and seeing the natural world is harder when living in the large cities. Therefore these cities are no longer the right place for humans to live. A primary target for major change is these large cities. There are a number of events being set in motion to make enormous cities redundant, to reduce their size and importance, and reverse the trend for urbanisation. Covid has encouraged home-working and the emptiness of large cities was initially shocking, but a middle way will emerge as people return to work. The potential is there for less pollution as fewer car journeys need to be made with home-working. People who visit their offices two or three days a week will not be commuting on the other days. There can be moderation with changes, it doesn't have to be all or nothing.

Large cities can continue to be the cultural and political centres of nations. They can become healthier and more open by creating additional parks and green spaces. In the past there were more people living in the countryside and a greater number of healthy middle-sized market towns. It is an imbalance to have populations crowd into cities in order to work to live, leaving the countryside empty of people. This kind of population shift is relatively easy to make, and would be easier if governments supported them with their policies. Some countries will fare better at this than others.

When Covid-19 is finally no longer a problem on Earth, people will not remake the cities exactly as they were in 2020. Given a free choice there will be changes in work and housing, fewer commuters and smaller offices with greater flexibility to work from home, and more understanding and help for families where both parents hold down jobs. It isn't many decades since the large social economic shifts that stretched families to the limit. Today it is hard to find sufficient time to spend together as families and enough money so as not to worry about making ends meet. There is enough of both money and time, but they are not shared out equally. What affects one of you affects all of you and economic imbalance to the degree that it exists now is taking a heavy toll on all people. You are enslaved by economic policy.

13
Practicing Forgiveness the Atlantean Way

THERE was a special period of healing and forgiveness in the distant past, following the human race's loss of its homeland on Atlantis. The loss came about due to the actions of the ruling class on Atlantis, who had assumed control and forced the islands in a direction the majority of people abhorred. The survivors of the ensuing catastrophe took on the task of forgiving all of the rulers and their cohorts who had brought about the end of their long civilisation, all now dead and vanished with Atlantis. They did this so they could live without the burden of their resentment, anger and hatred, to release and let go of the shock and the pain. If they could not let go of this burden they could still sink under their hatred even after having survived the physical destruction of their land.

The Atlantean islands were the centre of human advances in science and culture, a civilisation that had lasted for approximately one hundred and forty thousand years, continually making advancements on its previous achievements. This incredibly beautiful land allowed humans to be creative and stretch themselves to the limits of their minds and hearts, right up until the end. The Earth provided for their needs and gave them space to learn what it was to be human. Until almost the end time there was a society that worked well, where everyone shared in the wealth of ideas and prosperity and people were happy in their lives. It was

47

all quite glorious, but Atlantis was lost before humanity was able to put the finishing touches to their learning and make their ascension. Their story is told in our book *The Downfall of Atlantis* by this author.

Atlantis was unique on Earth in its temperate location and natural gifts. As an island nation it was protected from the casual warfare present on the continents. We angels came and walked among the locals, instructing them in many ways, and always our lessons were filled with love and light. During all the many years of its existence Atlanteans listened to us and achieved great accomplishments. They lived their lives with great pleasure and by living joyfully maintained their health and strength. We taught them how to use universal life force energy, and to stay balanced and true by honouring the Earth as they had promised at the beginning of humanity's time here. All life here honours the Earth for giving them a home and providing everything they need for life. Humans have come to show their gratitude in many ways, but in Atlantis they were taught to set aside time for Earth healing circles and fill the planet with the light it needs as an offering of love. Joy is infectious, and they spread joy easily amongst themselves thereby keeping their minds and hearts open and free. For a long time disease was unknown and only came later as a by-product of the lack of love.. When love and joy were stolen from them and replaced with fear by the controlling hierarchies, everything began to fall apart.

The shipwrecked survivors undertook to forgive those who removed the love and joy from their lives and replaced it with fear and pain. They knew they had to forgive everyone whose actions led to the destruction of their beloved land in order to preserve their own well-being. To do this they fully opened their hearts and chanted a verse:

Today I stand on the earth and she is beautiful
Today I remember those who died in the sea
Today I feel only love for all of these people who were
me, are me, will be me
I weep for their loss until we meet again

Learning to create a forgiveness chant was a common practice in Atlantis, taught to all children so as to stay well and remain sane. To forgive another is something you do for yourself. This chant reminded them that they are all one soul and if they cannot love everyone as they love themselves they do not understand humanity, or their own portion of divinity. Without forgiveness they could be alive, but not living in joy. This is still true today. To live in joy is to live in the light of love, with open hearts and kindness for others. You can write your own forgiveness chants today.

After the destruction of Atlantis the people were scattered around the continents bordering the Atlantic Ocean. Some went all the way to the end of the Mediterranean Sea and landed in Egypt, causing a revolution in technology in that land, changing their society forever. Egypt is where the technological aspects of Atlantis remained the longest, while the spiritual practises lasted longer in the British Isles and Ireland. The average Atlantean was familiar with many aspects of technology and spirituality that are unfamiliar to us today. Atlantean research concentrated on the uses of energy from crystals and the Earth itself. These were clean sources of energy, enough for everyone. A deliberate misuse of energy damaged the large power crystals in an attempt to kill the Earth, swiftly leading to the destruction of Atlantis. We could not allow the Earth to die from an attack like this. Traumatised Atlanteans climbed out of their boats wherever they washed ashore to start over. For the most part these were fishermen or coastal farmers and their families. They were already reeling from the recent years of devastation from the final Wizard Wars which attempted destruction across time, space and higher dimensions to follow reincarnated Atlanteans whenever they were reborn. There are people alive today who still carry scars, spells, chains, and more in their auras from the final days of Atlantis. This threat only ended with the downfall of Atlantis. The refugees now had to heal and survive, and forgive.

Traumatised people have mental scaring, and these survivors knew more about healing than most people alive today, although they had not worked in any of the healing temples. They set a regular time for formal sessions of forgiveness, and made sure no one failed to attend and therefore retain their trauma scars. They could not carry the burden of hate and resentment against all of those who had brought their civilisation to a destructive end. They practised forgiveness until the scars were gone and they could begin to move forward. We tell you this because so many of you hold trauma scars today from difficult lives that did not really have enough love. Do you love yourself enough to forgive others? The more you feel they have wronged you the more you will gain from practicing forgiveness.

We are recounting this part of the Atlantean story now because we see the divisions between all humans, male and female, black and white, rich and poor. Wherever there is resentment or hate there is a need to leave it behind and start walking forward into a new future. The surest way to do this is by forgiving others. There is no one alive on Earth now who would not benefit from setting up a schedule of practicing forgiveness, where all you think about is releasing the wrongs, real and imagined, that have been done to you by forgiving these wrongs. If you focus on one person who has wronged you, in the end you will see your common humanity and that you are both splinters of one soul. Although you may have taken harm from someone's actions, you are now harming yourself by not forgiving that person. By separating the action from the person in your mind you can begin to find a way towards forgiveness. If you wish to call the hurt trauma, it certainly is trauma to a greater or lesser degree. Love follows forgiveness in a natural order as the person is allowed to rejoin the rest of humanity in your mind and be held in the love you hold for all people, including yourself. When we talk about laying down burdens that no longer serve you, forgiving others is how you can lay down some of the heaviest burdens. Could you schedule in a special weekly forgiveness session to heal yourself?

14

A Toxic Earth

A NOTHER crisis to raise its head will be increasing rates of infertility in human beings. The Earth is now holding so many devastating man-made poisons that their ingestion will sharply pull down fertility levels. Conceiving a baby will become much harder all around the world and as babies decrease and the elderly die the population will noticeably shrink. This will frighten everyone, even governments will wake up to the problem and they will wonder what the future will be like if they have fewer young workers to make the economy run as it did in the past. The planet is heading into a time of chaos and not everything will be as it was before. Your challenge is to create a workable future that does not repeat the mistakes of the past. This future way of life has always been possible if you could get fixed ideas and false beliefs out of the way. This is why we urge you to let go of everything that no longer serves you. From our point of view there are a great many beliefs that no longer have any value at all.

Up until the last one hundred and fifty years or so you were able to live and raise your children on a relatively clean planet. The air wasn't as poisoned, nor was the land or sea. You could eat fish, plants and animals that were healthy and free of chemicals. The research has been published showing the affects of air pollution in large cities on mental illness, and you are not able to restrict polluted air to just the cities even if it is at its worst there. Plants and animals share this poisoned air and soil with people. What could be more important than clean air and water to you? This is where you can begin to focus your efforts on cleaning planet Earth. Become aware of everything that affects the air and water and devote yourselves to counteracting the degradation that continues on a daily or hourly basis. Do it in your homes and wherever else you can. Some distressing problems, like high levels of mental illness, can be helped by lowering pollution. Not everyone's mental problems are solely down to air pollution, but pollution will still contribute a negative effect. Ignore talk about humans mutating and adapting to breathing poison, you don't have that much time left on the planet.

We see your end date as a window you are heading for, aiming to climb through and escape to the next level and have some new adventures, with all of humanity going together. What if we said a couple of years ago 2030 was the year to aim for, but it's now 2024? What would you do? The date is not set in stone and can be improved, pushed farther back, but even if it goes back to 2030, it's not that far away. All projections regarding the cutting down of poisonous emissions by governments seem to be talking about much later dates in the century, so you can't rely on your governments stepping in and rescuing the planet. You will have to find your own way to contribute and find your own group of like minded people who work the way you do. In our role as angelic guides we see this as the most important use of your time here on Earth, playing the role you chose before you were born, saving humanity by saving the planet.

What happened and how did the date move forward? This

happened very recently as the natural monuments and public lands were opened in the USA for fossil fuel drilling. You need these parks to keep the animals alive so they can re-colonise the chemical desert caused by today's farming practices. It matters very much having your native animals ready to be part of your environment as with only plant life, but no animals, land quickly transforms into yet another man-made desert. A man-made desert is unnaturally unfriendly to life, contrasting to the original natural deserts and their varied life forms. Earth had originally created a balance in the size and number of her deserts, and creating more and more of them simply disrupts the weather patterns and deprives people, animals and insects of land for living and growing food. Part of what you need to do about saving the planet is fixing what you have harmed, and more importantly to stop all harm to it immediately. You need to support those people who are listening and willing to act to save your home planet.

Where to start? We mentioned air and water; they go everywhere and touch everything. Clean air and water are necessary for life. Every time you can manage a carbon-free journey, then make your journey that way and reduce exhaust emissions. Any time the majority of people change their habits in this way there is the beginning of a tidal wave of change. This will be seen when you can step back and compare the before and after Covid worlds. To rearrange your lives to pollute less you will need to make many small changes, along with the larger ones such as moving jobs and homes. These small changes, many of which are to do with plastic, will cause the producers of plastic packaging and more to switch their productions. <u>If no one buys it they will stop making it.</u> Talk about these things with your friends, so they know what you are doing and why so that it can spread further. No one wants the planet to end, but there are many who will not lift a finger to change their lives and you are only able to change your own. Your friends will hear you when you explain why you traded in your polluting car for a cleaner one, or stopped buying some products. They may ignore the many discussions on climate change in the world, but they will hear you. It's important to stand up and not be afraid anymore, you will be talking to people who agree with you, but perhaps haven't thought seriously about it. Most of them will copy you if they can. Don't be a polluter and help end the madness.

We can see a day coming when there will be shopping strikes against some goods. This type of behaviour will swiftly stop production of some items and there will be a juggling and repositioning of products in their factories. They'll cease making the offending item or create a better version of it. Think of chemical agricultural products, so harmful to the planet and all life, these could be better if everyone stopped buying them and asked for something wholesome and natural instead. It takes many working together but there are more than enough of you who are willing to do this. You were all born to do this, it's in your hearts and souls. You are increasingly anxious as you see daily life becoming worse and worse, people are ready to change now and will respond to you. If you are not an organiser, promote other people's good ideas by talking among your friends.

You weren't born to leave it to everyone else and make no changes in your own way of living; after all, you picked up this book to read. There will be many who walk blindly over an environmental cliff edge leaving all the changes to be done by others, but you are not one of them. You will do your best in difficult circumstances and you will be rewarded with peace of mind and peace in your hearts, knowing that when you were called on to act, you stepped up. Who can do more than that?

15

Planetary Regeneration

PLANETARY regeneration is a phrase that covers correcting past mistakes, such as the work today to restore deserts into healthy ecosystems. This is a fairly recent development, as in the past when suitable plans for regeneration were proposed they were ignored, just as most of the pleas for reducing pollution and cleaning the planet are still ignored. Interest in regeneration is only under consideration now as climate destruction derails nations' economies and societies and increases climate refugees. Planetary regeneration has resurfaced in the last few years with new plans to regenerate the Earth, many of which begin with the deserts. These are expensive plans depending on a great deal of funding before they can go ahead.

Deserts are great creators of climate and rainfall, or the lack of evenly spread rainfall across the entire planet. They have the ability to heat the air passing overhead, creating condensation for the rain to be dropped elsewhere. The increase in desert areas has led to increases in violent storms. In the past, vegetative growth and smaller desert size had the effect of softening storms by allowing rain to fall more frequently along the pathway rather than dumping it all at once at the final destination. Reclaiming deserts increases the green habitats in the local areas, while at the same time altering the climate in a wide area around the new sites.

A twenty five-year Chinese regeneration program has

created running rivers and farmland in a bleak desert on the Loess plateau in northern China, in an area almost the size of France. Using low-tech methods of planting trees on the hill-tops, terracing the steep eroded slopes, adding organic material to the soil and controlling grazing animals has led to the retention of water. This has allowed the desert to support life once again as farmland. You may be thinking: didn't farming turn the land into desert in the first place? We will have to see how the project is managed. If it is managed in a positive way there will be people there who are feeding themselves from their own land rather than struggling in refugee camps or the big cities. It's an important project, and, as it started twenty five years ago, it is providing an example for the rest of the world to study now. There are more projects making progress such as Africa's Great Green Wall, which aims to plant a line of eight thousand trees from Senegal to Djibouti, hoping to stabilise and reduce the size of the Sahara. The Sahara desert has grown hugely through man-made actions over the last two thousand years. It is a prime example of what happens when the animals are removed from the ecosystem; in this case it was the Romans who removed the animals to slaughter them in the circuses for entertainment. Northern Africa, once the breadbasket of Rome, turned into a desert.

There is a noticeable swell of interest in changing the climate back to what it was originally through regeneration. It took a while to get started, but now it is on its way. You don't need to push to get the movement going, simply work to keep it accelerating now as more and more people join together. People are taking it into their own hands to act, while the governments lag behind. We urge you to include "saving the planet" as part of your week. How you do this will vary from person to person, but there are so many ways to help that we are sure you will find your own way. Then include your friends and work on it together.

Always remember you chose to come to Earth at this very time, the time of this all-change-chaotic-mess of a crisis, because you have something to offer here and now. Join with others and enjoy working for the planet. You made a promise before you were born to do exactly that.

16

Balance in Your Lives

OCEANS are your great unseen deserts that are deteriorating at a furiously rapid pace. This is another area where destructive and careless practices are granted permission to operate by world governments. If you all remembered that you are one with all of life and the planet, there would be more cooperation in regulating destructive practices like bottom scraping, dredging and over-fishing. The dumping of toxic chemicals and sewage waste continues and, in addition, most of you pour chemicals into your toilets and wash your hair and clothes with products that are not biodegradable. Many shampoos are polluting. It's time to read labels and support the manufacturers of products that do no harm.

At the moment, many of the best products are made by smaller companies, started by people who want to offer you an alternative to polluting the seas. Imagine everyone buying these products while the large global corporations that do not listen fade away. Change is coming for a number of reasons, and you will be glad you supported local companies who have the expertise to continue making the cleanest environmental products. There are so many reasons to buy local, spending money with your neighbouring shops keeps the money in your area, not abroad; they pay their fair share of taxes and they can spend their money in other local shops, increasing the prosperity in your area. You may think you save pennies by buying from online retailers, but that is a false economy. They do not return money into your communities; they suck it out and bank it elsewhere. Whenever you are able, buy from your local shops and watch your community prosper. We have estimated that doing nothing more than shopping locally will alter the shape of the global economy (if everyone did this) within a year. It's the money tied up in the largest global business's bank accounts that impoverish everyone except themselves, including you.

It's beginning to sound complicated, for example telephones and broadband are from big companies, as is the petrol for your cars, the large banks and so on. Are we asking you to drop off the grid and use nothing that comes from a large corporation? Well, yes. It's difficult, but if you simply do the best you can in your own lives it will make a difference. You will only improve the planet by making the necessary changes and what seems impossible now may come into existence through public demand later. You are on a fast-track into the future now, never think that next year will be the same as this year. If you change something today it is possible you will change it again fairly soon, but just the act of changing makes all change easier. You become less attached to your choices and are ready to change once again when there is a new, better way to do something. Get used to flowing with this new energy.

A lot of what we are talking about may be considered a bit tedious at the moment and requires you to read a lot of fine print on the back of bottles and in any contracts. You will want to know who has the best environmental record when dealing with any number of corporations offering goods and services. The alternative to this is giving your money to people who are wrecking the planet and using your money to do so. If you are not happy to do that, then research online and read the fine print. Perhaps join a group that gives you a lot of that information as a member. You came here to heal the planet; you will find contributing to its destruction painful in body and soul.

We have been preaching about how to live your lives in this section of the book because it is the physical manifestation of your inner beliefs. Matching your actions with your words and thoughts brings together your mental, emotional, physical and spiritual bodies so that you are balanced and in alignment with yourself. It is surprising how few of you have these bodies in alignment and are balanced and effective in your daily lives. Working when you are not balanced is hard; a part of you is always struggling to find balance leaving less than one hundred percent available for the job at hand. Your reactions to the words and actions of other people are flawed as you swing back and forth searching for a point of balance to respond from. Much of what you see as "crazy behaviour" comes from people who are not balanced and have a lot of trouble just living their lives. These people share a soul with you and simply by balancing yourself you will be helping them. If you speak from a position of balance it will have a different effect on people who hear you. Some people won't be able to hear your words and they are in need of even more love and help. Do the best you can with those whom you do connect with. We encourage you to find and maintain balance in every way possible and speak up when it is called for, in defence of the Earth and other actions of light. Love is a great balancer, find unconditional love for everyone and everything, also importantly for yourself. Learn to disengage when something is the opposite of love and walk away to protect your own core balance. When you are strong return and have a conversation. You are one of those who are needed now to do this on behalf of everyone.

17

Help for Humanity

WHEN you look around today you often see many things that are disturbing and you have to work very hard to stay focused and positive, while holding and shining your own light. We angels are always here to support you in this every time you ask us for help, as we share your goals. Above all, practice keeping enough detachment not to get sucked into other people's lack of balance. You are the strong ones, look into your hearts for balance, look outside a window at the beautiful Earth and draw strength. Ground yourselves often by asking for the energy of the Earth to rise up your legs into your body and energy fields. You can't imagine what is coming next for humanity, the twists and turns, ups and downs of the next few years as everything corrects and rebalances. When the time of chaos is over you will be unscathed if you can remain detached and balanced. Your strength will support balance for the ones you love, helping them in standing up straight as everything is renewed. This is like house cleaning, what is swept out the door no longer has any place here.

About fifty years ago there was a sudden change in direction towards making the Earth uninhabitable for humans. Imagine a line going straight across a graph, and then suddenly dropping swiftly downwards. That was how the rate of unfavourable change looked to us from our perspective. At that very time the greater human consciousness made decisions to correct the problem, using its best option by deciding who gets to be born into a human body on planet Earth. There are many angels in human bodies on Earth right now, as well as elementals, star beings, and human/star being hybrids. We talked about some of these in our book *Stepping Through the Looking Glass*. Indigo and Crystal children are some who have been granted human bodies. They have been busy behind the scenes; they assist humanity without supplanting their leadership. They are not responsible for these problems and they will not fix them for you, but they love the Earth and they are happy to help her survive. They are on your side.

Other helpers are the increased numbers of elementals on the planet these days. The Earth creates elementals as she needs them, they are her trusted helpers. By creating so many, first to help with the work of rebirth in 2012 and now to help with the climate crisis, she maintains an army working for her. It won't be enough by itself to repair the damage, but they are knowledgeable and work non-stop everywhere there is environmental damage. It used to be an easier job being a planetary elemental, all about life and growth and beauty. Now they are experts at holding the dimensions together and keeping your world in one piece, along with fire fighting, flood damage repairs, keeping their beloved plants alive in droughts, and more. They work because they love the Earth but in some places, like the coral reefs, they are overwhelmed. They need all the damage to stop.

Finally, you really do have the best of your soul group here on Earth now, particularly the young people. Pay attention to who is saying what and you will find the leaders to follow with ideas and suggestions on how to turn this situation around.

They, in turn, need your support so you end up working together. They may be from another country, so keep reading and looking for people to learn from. You are also one of the best people here now and your support is worth having. Find your own way to contribute, please. There are many suggestions in our book *Guidebook to the Future.*

18

A Critical Mass

WHEN enough people alive today have genuinely pulled back from the production and consumption of planet destroying products and living ruinous lifestyles, you will approach a critical mass for change. There is always a critical mass somewhere, whether in the number of trees on the planet, or in viewpoints held in common. This critical mass for environmental change is just around the corner. Some of it will be brought on by the climate crisis, some of it by the coming decrease in world population. In the West and in other countries there will be fewer babies from climate restraints and environmental poisons. Once the world population begins to shrink because of fewer births there will be fast changes. At this point we do not see any particular differences in the lack of births between any of your continents. It looks to affect everyone evenly, even if for different reasons.

Population decrease is important and necessary to allow humans to pull back from the margins of their living spaces and to leave room for the animals to re-colonise their former ranges. Humans don't have to live on every square centimetre of the planet. There are any number of subsistence farms and even villages that now stand empty in Europe. Rather than see them as places that humans need to move back into, they are places that animals need to move back into. It's okay to return these lands to the original animal inhabitants. Some deserted villages in the Italian Alps are so high and remote that they have been abandoned because there is often better farmland further down the slopes.

Animals keep your world alive, along with insects and bacteria. One by one, people take actions that extinguish planetary life by buying pesticides and causing insect and animal extinctions. One by one you will reverse this trend by not buying pesticides and rediscovering how destructive insects used to be kept in check, perhaps by planting something nearby that they prefer to eat. It is the acres planted in monocultures where farmers feel they have no other choice than to buy pesticides. They don't have to plant single crops in fields. Again, *Guidebook to the Future* has a lot of suggestions on changing the way food is grown. This is one example of a change that will have a knock-on effect on many, many other aspects of Earthly life, from more insects to more employment as working people replace chemicals, creating a healthier planet for healthier people.

How close are you right now, at the time of writing in 2022, to achieving a critical mass of behavioural change amongst humanity? There are people who are waking up everywhere, with heads beginning to rise up and looking around at the way they are living and where it is leading. They don't need to look very far from home in most cases before deciding they can change their buying habits overnight. No products with chemicals, no inorganic food, no polluting cars anymore. They will say "enough is enough" and change their spending habits. You will see the shift begin from a consensus of critical mass, possibly as early as 2023. It would be better if it were now. It won't matter if it isn't everyone, as long as it is enough people. There are some people who will never change their ways and will be obstructive, but the world will change around them anyway.

Now the question is: if humanity waits until 2023 to make positive changes, do you have enough time left to repair the planet and reach human ascension? It will be close, but you can't affect this date in any other way than by making changes step by step. We certainly don't want you to wait; some people have to be the first to demand changes in order to bring new, healthy products to the market. Demand, once created, will find someone to fulfil it. You all came here to make these changes, so find a way to make it interesting and fun for yourselves. Do it with friends and exchange information. That will grow the rate of change exponentially as you work together.

We titled this section "Finishing on a High" because we see these incredible changes coming. We have talked here about how you live and how to change manufacturing by the way you spend your money and grow food. Furthermore, the Earth needs this now to bring relief to the oceans and soil, the atmosphere, and the poor, polluted human bodies which are now home to micro-plastics and chemicals. Many of the changes that are coming will begin in the summer of 2022 and will be across the spectrum of human activity, from politics and belief systems to economics. Some people will involve themselves in one thing, and others in something else, but they will all lead to changes, many of them very sudden and all happening at the same time. We angels see to the other side of these years of change and what we see is a beautiful planet once again, harmonious and peaceful with space for all the people and animals that belong here. Find your way to help bring this about with love.

Part 2: Finishing on a High

Part Three

Starting Over Again

19

Change Starts in Your Heart

IT LOOKS like an insurmountable task today to repair man's damage to the Earth and that many years are needed to clean and repair her. Much of the last section was to impress upon you the absolute importance of stopping all personal and harmful habits. Each time you fully change your habits you change the entire energy around consumption for everyone. It is the necessary first step without which the second step of cleaning and regenerating the planet is pointless, although there is now some overlap beginning to take place. It gives you a task that you can succeed at by yourself, in your own home, while you and others build the energy for greater changes. Every action matters because of the way energy is created and changed through action.

Energy is flow, and you will soon be creating a river of flow with others in a new direction. Each of you will be creating your own tiny streams that combine until you have reached the critical point where everyone will come and join you.

71

For some this will be simply a result of all the products and packaging being planet friendly with no other choices. Some people will actively create these changes. In the end you will all be living in the same way, for society-wide change. Some will be first and others will be last until you are all one. (Just like ascension!)

Let us assume you have reached the point where people are no longer harming the planet. This will partly come about through increased rates of death, thereby lowering the population level and the demands humans make on the Earth. It will also happen because people are more keenly aware of the changes that need to be made and they will outnumber the few that have been benefiting from exploiting every corner of the planet. Some of those businessmen will have died, but do not look for all the enemies of the planet to die and leave the way clear for regeneration. People will have to do the work they were born to do on behalf of the Earth in spite of the opposition from the old guard. The few wealthy will still hold the money, but others will find that by working together in many different ways solutions will be designed that won't require their funding. This will be a further economic blow to the system, as people will get what they want without going to the financiers. They will be cut out of the loop and lose their influence, which many of them love as much as money.

Sidestepping the wealthy in this way will have a balancing effect, not a disastrous one. Most people don't have the money to fund projects and do not expect to have millions given to them. They will instead work together to achieve their goals, each contributing their own money and labour to the group. The work will be on a smaller scale with a greater connection to the people who are doing the work locally. Small scale is all that is needed in the beginning, as again this will change the flow of energy in exactly the same way as when a person changes their consumption patterns. The last to join may be the ones holding all the money to contribute to a large project, perhaps with their name on it as important infrastructure in the long run. They won't be the first, but when everything is happening without them the wealthy will join in. They will be joining a system that has learned to get by without them and does not value the possession of money in the same way as in the past. It will be a big change. By changing peoples' perspectives of how much money they need, they will connect to one another in a new way, changing the goods and services they wish to buy, and reassess how much is enough. It will be harder to sell them what they have no use for in their lives.

Many people feel shut out in their national economies today, and so they are. We have talked in the past about the wage slavery that involves working very hard for just enough pay to live cheaply on, when there are often large profits in a business. There does not need to be the same pay for every person, but the highest paid and the lowest paid should not be so far apart in income. There is enough wealth on this planet for everyone to have a decent life. This has a lot to do with the way money is viewed and honoured, and a lack of love and compassion for all life. Turn it around, where love and compassion for all is honoured and then money will take a back seat. With love and heart placed over greed your world would change overnight.

To begin the change to a world based on love and compassion, we come back to all of you making individual efforts to create exactly that kind of world, and forming the small streams that lead to a large river of change. You have to change the energy first, every time, before you see physical changes. It's how change happens and once the river of energy is flowing in a new direction then it will be accomplished. In order to go backwards the same process will have to begin again by making individual changes leading in the old direction. Energy is everything; you yourselves are beings where the energy flow has slowed to the point where you have solid bodies. Energy is created through your intentions and your focus. If you focus on growing wild flowers for insects and talk to everyone you know about your passion for natural gardens they will be inspired by you to do the same. It's about passion and the desire to change the status quo, making the natural world a better place by caring for the little insects to help the birds, flowers and vegetable plants, lizards and fish. The entire world is dependent on insects, either eating them or being pollinated by them. You are the end user of these products and you have a great deal to lose by the insects' devastating drop in numbers due to pesticides and degraded environment. It happens when you do not love all the beings you share the Earth with and fail to take care of their home.

Change starts in the heart, when you say to all life "I love you enough to make a healthy home for you." "I love myself enough to fulfil my purpose in this lifetime by working for the Earth." Peace, beauty and harmony are a birthright for all life on this planet and when you participate in removing these by your lack of action, or the actions you take, you are complicit with those who destroy the planet, as if you have done the actions yourself. This is not who you are.

20

Love Can Fix Anything

A LONG time ago you lived in the forests, on the plains and on islands. You became specialists in survival in your areas and you always remembered that next year's meals were cultivated today. You caught the salmon after they had spawned and were heading downstream to die, and you left enough fruit and nuts on the trees to feed the neighbouring animals who helped you by planting the seeds for future trees. It was common sense survival knowledge, passed down through the generations where all life was lived together and there was food for all. Occasionally there were hard years, but nothing like the extremes you are witnessing now with the climate crisis. Don't try to become accustomed to extreme change but devote yourselves to rebalancing the Earth.

How does it make you feel to read about the salmon being caught after spawning and know that this is no longer the practice? Salmon have been caught swimming upstream before they can spawn to the point of vanishing, by the fishermen whose livelihoods depend on the salmon. This is the opposite of common sense and only greed could make this possible. To catch a fish swimming upstream in case someone else catches it! Now multiply this behaviour across forests, farmlands and islands. Greed limits the future by destroying today, taking for yourselves instead of the community. Are your local fishermen greedy? It's hard to see it that way, caught as they are in a low-pay profession trying to catch enough fish in depleted seas to make a living. What about the global corporate fish factories sailing the oceans, vacuuming up fish and stripping the ocean floors?

Fish are endangered today. This is one of the greatest losses your planet could suffer as fish swim through the water creating flow. They stir the water like a spoon in a glass. Fish are able to communicate with each other in their schools as they have a tightly shared soul, living a very different way from humans. Do you think fish don't realise what is going on? You need to stop the current methods of fishing and let them breed. They also require underwater reserves to have a safe place from which to breed and restock the oceans. If humans did this, then you could see the change in energy from selfishness to thinking in common about the future of all life. The energy stops being focused solely on people and by turning outwards starts the flow again. In every aspect of life on Earth there is energy and flow, or alternatively, stagnant energy.

Angels and some humans see energy flowing and see it flowing with light, or if it has stopped in a stagnant pool of darkness. There are ways to identify the energy in something even if you are not one of those who can see energy. You can tell what the energy is by what is happening in any situation. If you identify a situation that seems dark to you, then consider that the energy is probably stagnant. You can also *feel* when energy is not flowing with light. How do you go about changing a situation that strikes you as negative?

When looking to change the energy around a situation to make it feel right to you, it is necessary to allow for the possibility that you are in the wrong and yet still be willing to act. This means that you have to let go of the outcome and only act for the highest good of all. That way it will be for everyone's highest good, including yours. It's a relief to leave an outcome up to the universe and do your work free of judgement. You are able to lay down the burden of trying to find the right thing to do without having all the information, as you will never have all the information. By letting go of your attachment to the results you make space for something to happen that you may never have wished for in the short term. Some actions that you dislike may bring forth a reaction from others that you then see is the best for all. Knowing this helps you let go of all worry. When you work with the Divine by saying "I only want what is for the highest good of all" you have aligned yourself with love and the Creator. Whatever happens, you can be content with the outcome.

We recommend focusing on your chosen subject and sending light in the form of prayers, Reiki, Spiritual Healing, meditative and positive thoughts, etc. Do not give up too quickly and continue over the days and months until you see a change. We assure you that this is your best tool to change situations that seem wrong to you. Find some friends and join together at the same time so you have an exponential effect with your healing. If you have three people you are healing with the force of nine, ten people with the force of one hundred and so on. It's just how it works. Send a link upwards to the grid of ascended masters above the Earth, written about in our book *After We Die*. Connecting to this grid plugs you into one of the planetary energy sources of light, particularly helpful for smaller healing circles.

This is how energy can be changed, by people setting aside

some of their own time to altruistically help create the world they wish to live in. If you have an idea that you feel passionate about, then it is worth your while forming your own healing circle and focusing on it. Ask us (angels and beings of light) to be there with our help and we will be present.

Now is the time of healers and light workers. There has been an explosion in training over the past couple of decades to swell your numbers just for this planetary emergency. The few have become many and people are waking up to how close the end of the planet could be. Unfortunately approximately one third of these light workers have been lost to the conspiracy theories, which was never the original plan, making it even more important that the remainder step forward and act. Don't be afraid to look for and find the friends and acquaintances that will join you in healing circles. Perhaps you can join them in their projects? People are worried about the planet and are angry at the lack of action from world governments as there is so much to do and so little time. If you are an energy worker or healer you have a brilliant tool to start with that you can use from your own home. Some of you are meant to be working this way in organised, efficient groups, connected and communicating with each other and meeting regularly. Did you come here to work in this way? Not everyone has, but maybe you did. We talk about healers, but a church group that prays on a subject for the highest good of all is also very effective when praying together and not letting their minds wander. Prayers require concentration. These are tools for you to use and now is the time to start.

21

Reaching a Tipping Point

D O YOU remember reading in our first book *Planet Earth Today* about the original plan for humanity, when you arranged to live on Earth to have a very specific living experience? Humanity is here to remember it is a tiny part of God by starting from a place of complete unknowing, like a blank sheet of paper. The human race knows very well it is part of the Divine, as it has learned it many times before in many different ways, on a number of other planets. This stay on Earth is a simple relearning of who you are and so as not to make the task too easy, you made it extremely difficult for yourself by wearing a blindfold hiding the higher dimensions. For this experience on Earth you set the stakes higher than ever before because of the timing of this game in the overall age of the universe. A universe is timeless, yet it ages in the number and quality of the experiences of the many life forms present. It is a contained space we once described as being like a brown paper bag where you could open the top and look in to see the galaxies in their orbits around the centre. Whose viewpoint could that have been? Only those who realise they are part of God can look through His eyes from His perspective. There are more people who are able to do this every day.

Otherwise, for all practical purposes, this universe is sealed. There are many universes in existence, too many to count.

You have the outer edges of the paper bag to define your limits and you have the entrance and exit points in the very centre of each galaxy, not the centre of the universe itself. This is useful as it brings all beings closer to the energy of their central galactic suns, and on the other side of this sun is shining the love of the Divine Being that created all life. It is also the originating point where galactic waves of energy flow out to meet each star and planet. By having an access point, a peep hole, into the centre of each galaxy the Creator is able to help and send galactic energy waves of light in the way that is best for each at the time.

In our book *And I Saw A New Earth* we wrote about your planet being in the lead position for your galaxy. You are leading the rest of the galaxy into the universal constellations of spring and the remainder of the Milky Way follows behind you at the moment. The galaxy that leads the way into this new constellation leads the rest of the galaxies in the universe, so that you are leading all the other life forms in the universe across a line denoting a change in energy from the stillness of winter into the sudden growth of spring. That's a lot of change as you shimmer and renew yourself on the journey, first among equals. No wonder the entire universe is watching to see what happens here, on the planet that has existed on a knife edge for so long.

Humanity's experience or game on Earth has been difficult because of the decision made at the start to blindfold yourselves and forget entirely who you are. You are struggling to finish this game in light, by showing that you love everyone and the planet without any exceptions. Humanity is close to achieving this by almost being ready to take the final few steps. Showing that you are repairing the planet will be enough and not everyone will have to do this. Ascension will follow if enough of you come together forming a critical mass and changing the way people behave and treat others, including the planet and other life forms.

No one will step in and do this for humanity but a lot of help is here for you. Your contribution to the learning experience of the whole universe is recognised, by bringing everyone closer to God. This is hard for you to see, almost impossible in fact, but this is why there are people channelling angels, aliens, ascended masters, etc. There is help at hand; whatever you need there is someone to help you manifest it. This is important, because the work they do for you in the energy fields of Earth you cannot do, only when people ask for this help does the work get done. The building and healing of the planetary energy grids is done on your behalf by others, often because a living human being asked for this help. You have so much power to use in an informed way, by using your intuition and reading all kinds of information by everyone from channels to scientists to fiction writers. It's how you will complete your time here.

At this time there are a great many light workers on Earth, holding a higher vibration for the entire population. This was always intended for these times. The way many light workers use healing energy may be unknown to you as there are different ways of holding light. That is also important right now, to combine the diverse practices and have them work together in harmony. Exposing darkness to light, shining a beam into dark corners heals the sickness and corrupted energy hidden there, the unhealthy substance of humanity. You are moving forward daily, progressing at a speed you can't see, without any way of knowing if or when you are getting close to the tipping point of real change. All you can do is keep going and build up the numbers of people who are changing their habits.

22

Working in the Fifth Dimension

HUMANITY is one small soul in a universe filled with life, and as such is valued as part of the whole. It's a difficult perspective to see yourself as one of so many, a speck of dust among other specks of dust, but that is how humanity fits into the life of the universe. If humanity wasn't there, the whole of life would not be the same. People belong in this universe, created by the Creator Who Loves Us All and no matter how this game of life on Earth ends you will always be loved. We feel you deserve better than to finish in darkness, when you have increased the flow of light for other souls across the universe. You will one day finish your time on Earth and either go with the planet to a higher dimensional experience filled with light and opportunities or you will find yourselves without a home looking for a new planet to begin again. There are no guarantees you will find one as consummately skilled as the Earth in managing difficult games. She has learned how to do this to perfection. As we have said earlier, many planets are waiting for the end of the universe now without troubling themselves by changing tenants. It's that close in time to the end, measured by experiences. Our book *After We Die* covers this subject in greater detail.

Just as humanity is a single great soul among the countless billions of souls, you are one splinter of this soul among the billions of people on Earth. You are part of the whole of life on Earth and your individual actions make a difference when you initiate the energy to take your actions. Each of you creates the Earth's environment this way and each of you would be missed if you were not here, for better or worse. Once you incarnate on Earth you contribute to the whole of humanity with your actions. Our advice and guidance to you is don't work alone. Find like-minded people and work together. The amount of change you can create with a group of friends, a large organisation or charity is exponential in size. Some of you may be hesitant for any number of reasons about contacting others or inviting others to join you, but achieving your dreams will be more likely if you work inside a group. You support each other and bring different knowledge and points of view to expand the group mind. The energy work you undertake expands your unconscious minds. You all grow together in wisdom, strength, and balance.

Today you are able to connect with others over the internet and we have blessed many of these healing circles with our presence. We make sure that you are experiencing the same energetic connection that you would have when meeting together in person. Your circles can now be vast and powerful with many angels and other beings of light joining people around the globe in their healing work. All the darkness present in the internet is somewhat offset by these online circles. These are giving you the chance to participate in a field of energy greater than any you may have joined in the past and people's hearts are opening because of them. We encourage you to find a way to participate in a circle that matches your interests. Some of the larger Reiki self-treatment circles are raising the vibration of all humanity by simply self-treating together in an online group. The balance of light is pulled ahead by people working together, as the dark pulls back in other ways. This is your end game, will the light increase until the balance is tipped against the dark side? What is your personal role in this?

We wish to explain a method that works for church goers, healing conferences and gatherings, retreats, etc. If you state your intention to heal and leave the invitation energetically open to others in the room, you will be joined by the higher selves of those who are willing. They probably won't consciously know, but if they are unwilling they will ignore the invitation. If you look for a space in the program where you are less engaged and just listening, you can set your intention to heal for a while. The important thing is to act, and once you specify "for the highest good of all" you will include those who wish to join and allow others to exclude themselves. Pick somewhere like the Amazon rain forest, for example, and let the energy flow to help.

We are suggesting different options for you to try and it is our sincere hope that you will set aside some of your time and find a regular way of healing with the light. If you sit in a church service every week you can consciously ground up (see appendix) with Earth energy, then let your prayers be for the health of the Earth for the highest good of all, or a specific location. The healing will take place while you are connected to both the Earth and the congregation you have joined that day. The congregation is a unit during the time it sits together and manifests its prayers very effectively when led by a speaker. You will have to consciously invite (not out loud) the congregation to pray for the Earth and also thank everyone for their support. Prayers for your planet are appropriate and belong in every service of worship around

85

the world. With a large group and a heartfelt prayer the love can be quickly delivered, for instance by holding the prayer in the front of your mind during one hymn. We recommend this because music will help the energy flow. Those who are unwilling will not have joined you, but there will be a majority in every church who will wish to connect and help with what their subconscious mind is aware of taking place. It is their higher selves who will have joined you, and you will have led the prayers by specifying them for the highest good of all.

This is working on a higher level, energetically and deliberately. If you start working like this you will find it is easy and natural, and you will find ways of working that are new to you and without disrespecting the group you are with. This is part of what is happening when you hear that people are moving into a five dimensional world. You will be using skills that are set outside the three dimensions of height, width and depth. You all have a lot to offer, and by changing the energy you will be changing the physical world.

23

How to be an Effective Healer

NOW YOU have an idea of how you can work with the higher dimensions in a practical way, by connecting to beings of light and the planet's energy grids and asking for help. If you could see these beings or grids everyday then they would be in your dimensions. If you can only see them when you are in a meditative or altered state then they are in one of the higher dimensions. You may have thought living in a five dimensional world would be very different, hoping perhaps to see and hear all the higher dimensional beings around you. This has an increasing possibility of happening now and it should become easier, it just takes steady practice. To see angels and elementals it is easiest when you are in a meditative state. You can do this sitting still or when you walk alone through trees in a walking meditation, staying very present and observing what you see around you. Go outside into natural locations where the elementals live. They respond to people who heal the Earth and you can ask for their help with this, or healing for yourself. They are not beings of light, they are simply themselves. Angels, on the other hand, are beings of light, are present everywhere and ready to help you at all times. The more you ask for their help, the more you will be in contact with them and get to know them, how they feel, look and sound. The final outcome on Earth is as important to them as it is to you.

There is also an element of practicality in living with an awareness of five dimensions. You are not used to seeing your world with these extra dimensions and if you saw the crowds of higher dimensional beings that naturally exist in your world it would be disconcerting. Every walk in the countryside would be full of elementals ignoring you and going about their own business, distracting you while you are talking with friends or family. It can be a bit overwhelming for humans. That is why your most successful psychic viewers work on demand, in that they ask to see something specific for a reason, or even simple curiosity. If they want to see which elementals are present and what they are doing they tend to look and then shut down the picture. Hearing every conversation of elementals and angels would be a babble of overlapping sound, you would soon wish it to stop. Again, asking when you have a question and listening for a short time works well. If you had started life by seeing and hearing all of these beings it would be different, but it would be a huge adjustment to see them all the time now.

What can work better is to hone your senses so that you start to feel when they are close by. A large elemental like a dragon or giant will suddenly make you think that there is something very large close to you. At that point you can practise your higher dimensional sight by turning around and feeling in which direction to look. You can also feel their emotions; this can also work well with angels. They share your range of emotions and you can feel these when they are nearby. Sometimes you can feel their excitement or sorrow, and feel their laughter rather than hear it. These are small starting points that can lead you much, much further on if you practice. Being in tune with the higher dimensions can help with warnings, such as taking another road to avoid trouble. This could be a familiar feeling to you, but how many people appear to have no idea of what is happening around them? This type of help is coming to you from your spirit guides all the time, as nudges to correct you on your path. If you always followed their guidance and stayed close to your chosen path, what an amazing person you would be as you learned only the lessons you needed to learn and avoided the dead ends and disastrous shortcuts! We who are your spirit guides care for you and advise you, but we can't make you take any steps you don't wish to take.

For most of you the fifth dimension is the real place where you practice your healing. With your prayers, Reiki or other form of healing you are changing the energy around a subject, softening it so it can be ready to flow. A stuck situation will require this kind of energy to begin any change. This is why you need to know how best to use your good intentions and the time spent focusing on a problem. If your aim is to heal, then doing it for the highest good of all will have the greatest impact. You may think you might not like the result or that you have a very specific result in mind, such as getting the job you just interviewed for, but the highest good of all will cut through to the core of any problem. It could be a very bad job for you, and not getting it could be for your highest good. When you heal in this way the entire problem starts shifting in the best direction. If you impose your own desires then your healing may glance off the target rather than make a change. This is a very common problem with healing and prayers, so learning to trust the result that is for the highest good of all will make you a very effective healer.

Healing for the highest good of all also lets you combine with others to heal the same subject, without confusion or competition from different ideologies. Take politics for example, can you imagine organising a single healing group where half the people voted for one party and the other half voted for the other in an election? Yes, if it is for the highest good of all. You can send light or prayers on behalf of all citizens that way, and let go of any attachment to the outcome, only wishing for the best result for all. We don't mind this type of subject, but there are more important problems on your horizon at the moment. If you want to heal politics, heal the people first with love to create the greatest force for change. Love for the wellbeing of all people for the highest good of all.

We wanted to be clear about how to be an effective healer because you have limited time for the amount of help and healing that the planet needs today. You could heal or pray from dawn to dusk to help the Earth. How much better it is to combine with others and work effectively. There are groups out there looking for more healers to come and join them or you could always organise your own. The time has arrived for the healers and light workers to make a difference and this is what is different today from the past. Healing is an aspect of love and love can fix anything!

24

How Do You Heal a Rainforest?

HEALING and prayers are how many of you will work to improve some of the biggest planetary problems on Earth today. We are speaking of the polluted atmosphere and oceans, deforestation, land degradation, etc. These are long term problems and are in need of as much help as possible right now to make the necessary changes.

Let's say you wish to focus on healing trees in tropical forests. This would include the entire belt around the Earth that suffers the most rapid damage from humans, from the Amazon basin to the palm tree plantations in South East Asia. We will state that from our perspective the best solution would be an immediate halt to the logging and ripping out the old growth forests. They have the richness to provide homes for Earth's fellow residents, the birds, animals and insects. You could organise a group to send healing to stop destroying the forests immediately, for the highest good of all. The energy you send will feed into this problem, to begin changing the energy around it and loosening the rigidity that resists change. It can smooth the pathway to finding alternative employment for those who have been hired to work there. Perhaps at the same time there will be some large firms that escape punishment or fines, but somehow that turns out to be for the highest good also. As the healing energy arrives, what is taking place in the forests will begin to change.

The healing energy may also find its way to inspiring people to lobby for the end to destruction, perhaps by writing letters and blocking access to the trees. Scientists may be inspired to invent a substitute for the rain forest products, cheaper and easier to obtain than the actual natural substances. Politicians may realise it will make them more popular if they come out in favour of saving the rain forests and institute boycotts of countries and products. The various climate summits could be better supported and help the rain forests through an international consensus. In the forests this energy can support and heal the life that is still there, calming down the soil and rebalancing the ecosystems. You can do all this from your home, working together in groups that make you many times stronger.

How long would it take to make this amount of change happen? If people worked together, with a large number of different groups meeting every day in multiple countries around the world so the healing is continuous across the time zones, about three months.

Joining or starting weekly Earth healing groups will have this kind of effect on the health of the planet, including humanity. You are trying to live healthily on a dying planet, why not try living on one that is vibrant and alive instead? Humans have a race memory of what it was like when the Earth provided for all your needs. She can rebalance and provide for life again.

Every book we have written with this author has included the subject of Earth healing and as each year has passed it has become more and more urgent. You have any number of helpful instructions on how to do this, you have the power in your hands and now you need to act. Forget what anyone else is doing, what are you doing to help? This aligns with your hearts and you will find the work fulfilling when you donate some of your time in healing. It is the great challenge of your lifetime, and people will need to do this in spite of the inactivity by their many world governments. Don't look to them for help until they are forced to by the actions of the people. There is much they could have been doing for years but they failed to take action, it's up to all of you now.

25

Creating Emotional Capacity

ONCE upon a time there was, quite simply, the most beautiful planet in the galaxy. It was blue and green, temperate and welcoming to many forms of life. It was lush with plant life and the seas were filled with whole communities of water beings and fish, as were the skies. There was music in the skies from the birds and from the sound of the wind in the grasses and leaves of trees and from the crashing of waves on the shores. Earth was made to provide a place for every being to live their lives in comfort and sufficient food, allowing each and every one to contemplate the reason they were here at all. The interweaving lives of these beings created flowing energy, there was never any stagnancy and all was easy and light. Humanity was present here when Earth provided this form of living with no restrictions or constraints. You lived differently then, with more joy and pleasure, never bored or overworked and able to be with the people you loved. Your days were spent singing and gathering the food that the Earth offered to you. You did not settle in the parts of the planet where it was difficult to find food for yourselves; those places were occupied by animals and insect life that were suited to those areas. Everyone had enough without having to work too hard. The vibrancy of the Earth itself fed into your bodies and your lives so you lived longer, much longer, with better health, all the time surrounded by loved family members.

So what happened? We have covered this material in the *Downfall of Atlantis* and *Planet Earth Today*, but let us remind you that there were no constraints on how you could have chosen to learn that you are part of the Divine by taking part in His plan to learn about Himself through experiencing life in many different forms. You chose to experiment by living in every form of civilisation and you have tried every kind of variation to learn these lessons. Humanity chose to wear a blindfold to the higher dimensions, thereby making the lesson as difficult as possible. You are actually finished on Earth except for one final thing, and that is to put everything back the way you found it.

Fortunately, the greater human soul has found ways to alter how the game is running here and you have the tools to hand. It is calling people home when their time is up and although a global pandemic is pretty awful, some people have found it a quick transition from this life to the next. This is the important aspect of the Covid-19 pandemic, that for those who forgot how to die, or were afraid to die, the virus has helped them cross the threshold between life and death. You will all cross this threshold one day and it's better if it is easy and without a painful struggle. You are not entitled to life for a certain number of years, only until you complete your purpose in life.

In the past you would have returned to the greater human soul and after a rest period you would have returned as a baby with a new purpose. That's all changed now. Some of you will continue to do this, but there are a great many others who can rest, recombine, and say "I did my part." When we say "recombine" we mean that all the souls that had splintered to fill more than one living body, and many were filling between ten and fifteen bodies at once, could now become one soul again. This is an important point; splintering one human soul into that many bodies is how you have filled the world with billions of people. It also explains the many lives lived in poverty. If you had a fifteenth of your soul, how would you feel about lacking the requirements for physical life, as you are missing a lot of your actual self? There are many of these people living on Earth at the moment, although there are many others with one soul, one body.

Filling the Earth with billions of people was a good way to give you all a chance to see your oneness. So many people, some so destitute, everyone so different from you and the way you were raised and live your life now. Are you able to see yourself in them? Can you share with them to make their lives easier and treat them with love? This is the challenge of being part of the human family. The other major challenge is planetary stress and bringing a halt to the pathway that leads to the destruction of the Earth. Your challenge was always to realise you are a tiny part of God, as is every other life form here. They are you and you are them, all one together. All the different people living wildly different lives was meant to happen, and you are meant to stretch yourselves to love your neighbour as you love yourself and care for them as you would wish to be cared for yourself. Life has turned a corner on Earth now, and the people who are staying here and the people who are going home are beginning to separate. The ones who have done the hard work by living in more than one body are leaving in the greatest numbers first, relieved to bring their soul separation to an end. The others will find it easier to hang on a bit longer and work for the planet and humanity using their wisdom and their skills. Many of those leaving first will be in their twenties, thirties and forties.

The population levels over the next ten years will drop and the Covid-19 virus begins this process by creating the emotional capacity in your lives to deal with death. It was never supposed to kill great numbers of people, but it was to start the process in a gentle way. Deaths from the climate crisis will be harder to prevent, but will offer you the chance to show compassion. It will be most effective to help others through Earth healing to slow and repair the existing damage in order to save lives, or at least slow the loss of life. If you are supporting climate destruction through your taxes then why are you allowing that to happen? Find a way to change the status quo.

The human population of the planet will decrease and will begin migrating from threatened countries to safer ones. Many will die because of the climate crisis. You killed some of the Earth's other non-human residents and they are now extinct. We see your destruction of the planet as a bizarre form of extinction as you reduce the temperate areas in which you are able to live, and that people are prepared to keep doing this and never stop. It is incomprehensible to the other life forms here, as you sit in your house on fire and watch it burn around you, having set the fire yourself. Do you have to die in great numbers in order to change? It's the new human game plan, one that is aimed at reversing the damage. When it begins, remember that as everything changes, the population levels on Earth will be one part of that change. The life you have is eternal, and when the physical body you inhabited on Earth is at its end, your soul will live on. Your immortal soul will become part of the mega-soul of the planet and all life on her (written about in *After We Die*). When humanity has

has reached the point of ascension you will join with the Earth and the other life here and head into the future through the planetary gateway with the rest of the solar system following behind. Then the fun will begin!

26

More Change to Come

THE PLANETARY gateway mentioned in the first part of this book is not the end of the universe or the great return to Source. It is simply a huge change in the way the Earth will exist. You are on solid ground here at the moment, or are you? What you see as solid Earth for your feet to walk on is part of a complicated relationship between how you experience the flow of time here and your lifespan on the planet. Consider the rocks, they flow and it feels fast enough to them, sub-ducting under continents and causing changes that affect even swift-living beings. The Earth is energy that has slowed enough to appear solid to you, and also thin enough for the rocks to feel they flow. You look at a mayfly and think about it only living for twenty-four hours and how short its life is, but it is a whole life to them. Species do not measure time or flow in the way humans do. If the Earth raised the speed of her vibration just a little you might feel the ground is less solid under foot. This is happening now and will increase as she goes through the gateway.

There are some people, mostly the young, who are sensitive to the changes in vibration and feel the preparations for the planetary ride through the gateway. Some of this is created by relaxing their gender roles, a fact that is alarming some of the older generation. Those who are experiencing life as flow will not be the same people as those who are solid, lacking the quickness to move with the ever-changing events. The division is widening all the time between these two types of people. It's important to look ahead and follow where the young are leading, and help them with your love and understanding. Not everyone will do this and the pioneers of living fluidly will have a hard time in many societies. You need to accept that they are expressing themselves in this way at the exact right time to let you all move forward with the planet. They are an example of the best of you, brave and sensitive to the way the energy is changing around them, and fitting their lives to it. We wrote more about transgender people in *After We Die*.

These days you may wonder if you can keep up with the changes taking place around you as they arrive faster and faster. You don't feel particularly fluid perhaps, or don't know if you could be flexible enough to go with the new flow as wave after wave of energy and change bear down on you. What is the best way to live if you are no longer feeling young? We see the older generations as important in their ability to hold the energy and steady the pace of change. This is never about going backwards, it's about grounding the energy into the planet and yourselves, letting it fill you and change you in a quieter way, step by step. The Earth healing groups are a perfect way to contribute to the progress of humanity and the planet as it prepares to go through the gateway in the not-too-distant future. Earth is also changing step by step, and you can consider your required changes easy compared to hers! You are in a state of flow when you are holding energy as it changes every day and by letting it pass through you, then filling yourself again the next day with fresh energy. It is a deliberate action, and many older people have had decades of practice working with energy and can continue doing so in their usual way. For others, you can start now. Reiki is a daily practice of self-treatments leading to steady change. Regular prayer for the highest good of all aligns you with the flow of change, as does Spiritual Healing and other healing modalities. It's important to pick one that suits you and start this phase of self-healing and planetary healing, and take action. Universal energy is accessible through many different methods depending on where you live and who you can find to teach you.

You may be wondering about those people who refuse to alter their beliefs and dig in their heels in resistance. They certainly exist on your planet, and many of them could be your loved ones. Some of these people will change because they live with you and feel your energy change and it happens gradually, quietly. Others will not change, and rather than worrying about them just be sure you are doing your job to the best of your ability. Everyone on Earth has a purpose and we do not recommend trying to guess why some people are here. It's a waste of your time, simply keep moving forward yourself.

When the Earth leads the other planets of this solar system through the gateway it will not be THE ascension we have all been talking about. She will have to be ascended herself first, so the planet will ascend to combine you together into the one mega-soul made up of all the life on Earth and then she will move forward with you as one. You will no longer be the greater human consciousness; you will be much, much more than that. You will assimilate all the knowledge and experience of every life lived on Earth from bacteria to whales and you will finally understand the greatness of your game plan here. You will see how humanity had the inspiration to create such a difficult learning experience with the full cooperation of the Earth and how you managed to pull it off in spite of a high level of danger and risk. We watch, we help and we applaud you. You simply need to drop everything else and put the Earth back to the way she was when you came here.

Part Four

Dawn of the Endless Day

27

On the Brink of Change

WE HAVE given a lot of practical information to help you start changing the way you live now. Every time your purchases are more planet-friendly and every change you make in the way you live grabs hold of the energy and twists it in a new direction. By doing this you are refusing to drift in someone else's polluted and filthy stream and stop contributing your own mess to it. Instead you stride away looking for a clean stream to float in and work to maintain its health. Other people follow you and your stream becomes larger and swifter flowing, creating the new reality. The other filthy stream shrinks as fewer people choose to contribute to its pollution. Without some of you examining labels and changing your purchasing habits none of this will happen. It's safe to lead the way and there are plenty of jobs to do.

While planetary clean-up is getting underway there are a number of other things happening behind the scenes energetically. Practical steps release and drive the energy

103

forward to make the ascension changes. Actions are the engines pushing energy down hundreds of pathways, some on Earth, while others stretch out beyond the solar system. Humanity has an audience far beyond this galaxy, beings with their fingers on the pulses of living energy who are able to feel the tiniest changes. They've been watching and waiting for a number of changes to take place on Earth. Most importantly they are looking for unity, for the understanding that you are all one, that "other people" are you, your own reflection in a mirror. When you realise you are all one your behaviour will change toward each other and they will feel the energy of love as you wrap your hearts around every living being. These universal beings are waiting to feel unconditional love and compassion coming from Earth. Their focus on the Earth brings love from the universe to all on the planet, many of whom have had a very hard time learning what love is and to love one another. Feeling the health and wholeness of Earth will alert them that their entire universe is on the brink of change.

We are speaking here of angels, of advanced civilisations on ascended planets, of demons, of beings in physical bodies, of souls who have never had bodies: that is the entire consciousness of life in a huge universe. Families of souls in the universe have followed their own pathways to the light and now they are turning to look behind to see where you are. Your place has often been in the lead, and other souls looked to you for help and guidance in their games. You have inspired many successful and daring living experiences across time and space. Humanity is trusted to act on behalf of the light, as a soul of light. You have always taken seriously this role of bringing others to the light, through your integrity and adherence to the rules of any game you set up. Honesty in all things is at the core of humanity. You are aligned with Truth and Light, so take care that when you choose to walk down a road paved with lies that you are able to find your way back. You are lied to continually on your planet. Because the human soul is one of the brightest souls in the universe, whenever you deliberately align yourself with darkness and lies tiny cracks appear as you try to hold to a path that is not true to your soul. Many of your mental health problems these days can be traced back to any acts or beliefs that are the opposite of truth and light. When someone is "cracked" they have lost their ability to function in the world today, sensitive souls are not always able to cope with the confusion and darkness of lies.

The universe is familiar with humanity; there has always been a lot of bounce and style in the human nature. You have always been able to hold your own and attracted plenty of attention in the past. The other beings in the universe hold their hands out to you now, willing you to catch up with them and join together as they ready themselves for the next step. The goodwill for humanity is palpable. What these other beings also feel coming from the Earth is the potential for massive, rapid change. On the one hand they can feel the stuck energy that continues to allow the polluting industries and forest destruction, and on the other they feel flowing energy like cracks in a dam ready to break loose and unleash the flood waters. They are preparing themselves for a surge of light when this happens, when the energy that is piling up behind the dam breaks through and changes everything. Most of the people on Earth are behind that dam pushing for change, while the few who are profiting from the status quo are trying to keep the dam intact to maintain their power and wealth.

This kind of energy surge is similar to super-novas and stars. What do you imagine happens to the energy when a star explodes? There are universal and galactic ley lines that exist to channel that much energy as it pings planet after planet and star after star. This energy supports life and growth wherever it touches, and life is what the universe is about. It is also a gift of light. The soul of the star is not dead; it has the option to return again as a new star when it is ready. We can recommend looking at the beings inside your Sun. Ley lines and acupuncture meridians are energy highways, and you will only see them when you can see energy. That day is approaching for many of you. Otherwise you can usually feel them in your bodies if you train yourselves with practice to recognise what it is you are feeling.

The Earth is not a star, nor will she explode physically as that is not what planets do. They can be torn apart by gravitational forces as once happened to the sister planet that existed between the Earth and Mars. The Earth has always had her own important role to play, which made her vulnerable to attack from the dark angels that are our other halves. As the third planet out from the Sun she had bodyguards stretching out to the rim of the solar system, necessary in a universe of polarity. Uranus fell to attack a long time ago and circles the Sun on its side. There are no longer any living elementals on that planet. The rest of the solar system is intact in your three dimensions and the old threats are diminishing as the universe moves forward.

One of the greatest changes for you is the departure of Melchior, who wrote an interesting chapter in our first book

Planet Earth Today. Melchior, as the Archangel of Darkness has the job of bringing everyone back to the Creator Who Loves Us All, just as do the angels of light. His role was to let beings learn through misery and despair, which is also a pathway to God. We prefer joy and bliss. He and his team have been behind most of the misery on Earth, and his job was made almost too easy by the blindfold to the higher dimensions that you all wear. You will be familiar with his methods as fear and lies were his chief tools to deceive you. He left Earth in 2020 and took his team with him.

Melchior has begun his withdrawal from the universe, planet by planet, galaxy by galaxy to return to the Creator and rejoin Him as a part of Himself. He is packing up on a number of planets now. The Creator, who is a reservoir of ultimate and enduring love, is a whole being and includes everything there is. He includes darkness without hating, but learns who He is by experiencing the entire range of life, light and dark. He is the Source of All, including the source of darkness. Melchior is focusing now on bringing these lessons back to Him and it is a big job. All angels are beings of love and Melchior is respected among us by his obedience to his role no matter how it made him feel. His purpose was fulfilled over eons as he ingeniously created darkness on planet after planet. One day we will all be one again - until the next universe forms.

Therefore, on Earth today you are primarily dealing with the darkness in men's hearts. Or should we say minds? It is a great sadness for us that although you are all beings of light at heart you have ignored what you are able to feel and lived through your minds as if you were apprentice demons. Some of this is Melchior's doing as he was able to place a small block into the centre of the brain of most of the world's population. This small energetic object, like a grape, was able to block the heart and put it in a cage while the brain took over. It was the contact point for Melchior and he turned them all off when he left the planet like flicking a light switch. With frozen hearts humans were able to rule the planet as he wished.

Melchior's absence is a deliberate response to the human soul's plans to bring it's time here to a successful finish in light. You have reached a significant end point. With the demons gone and without their energy driving the darkness forward, much of what is dark will deflate. This lack of energy will be unattractive although few will use those words. Those empty human shells in governments will flounder, although some may yet find their hearts. There could be hard times ahead for some of these people. You have always had the right to be treated with love.

This change in energy has been brought about by the invitation to the Covid-19 virus. It was the first step demonstrating a serious plan to do a hard and difficult job in order to end your time here in light. Melchior pushed until he didn't need to any longer; he pushed you to take action.

28
Last Words from the Archangel of Darkness

ARCHANGEL Melchior has by now laid claim to half of this universe of polarity. He has approximately the same number of planets as we do on the side of the light, only considering those planets which have now settled for the light or the dark. As there are almost no planets left to choose either the light or the dark he is moving ahead to his next role, that of marshalling his planets to return them to Source. Melchior has the following to say about his timing for leaving the Earth.

"I left the Earth entirely in 2020 with my team, and slowly cleared them away beyond the edge of your solar system. I picked my time to leave based on maximum hate levels, so that hate would not diminish too quickly without my presence and energetic support. Since my absence the hate vibration pours forth from humanity. I have finished my job here. If you are able to change this vibration to love you are extraordinary light workers. As my vibration inevitably drops, you will find it easier to influence the change from hate to love.

At this time I am consolidating my planetary successes to bring them into alignment with one another. Once in alignment they will move as one toward the Creator when He calls for them. Marshalling my planets is one of my roles.

The Earth is excluded from my group for now. She and her living residents and the angels of light fought back tooth and nail and managed to maintain the presence of enough light, always pushing back against me. I have left, but I can always come back, and I will if I can add the Earth to my possessions.

At this time many loose ends are being tied up across the universe. There are few places left that have the potential to change for the dark or light. When I saw what humanity was prepared to do by dying in large numbers from covid-19, I called it a day and left.

Wherever my planets are in the universe I will take them through my own set of planetary gateways. On the other side of these I will align them for passage Home. This will be happening in your gateways also, marshalled by angels of light. The passage of Earth through the gateway is more than dimensional shifting; it is also a change in direction. Humanity will not wait long to begin flowing into its own alignment to God. The alignment of life will be like a stream of atoms flowing back to Source in the great in-breath, as all become one together in bliss, peace and fulfilment. Every soul in the universe has almost finished learning now and we wait only for a few planets like Earth. Shine your light and it will happen more quickly. I'm looking forward to the completion of this round of games."

The Earth will move through a gateway and meet the planets who have been waiting there for a very long time, giant, aged planets. When they chose to walk through the gateway they were finished with their lifetimes of hosting other souls. They were not as young and bright as the Earth is now and they felt ready to rest and wait for the end of time in something that feels like a train station, from whence they could journey onward easily. They each walked through alone so long ago they barely remember the bustle and energy in your dimensions of the universe. When you arrive they will be very happy to see the Earth with her vitality and physical energy. Earth will shift to a higher level whilst dropping much of her solidity and everything else she no longer needs. This process has already begun. On the other side she will be able to use the released energy from lightening her load to consolidate her growth and change. She will need to be this new version of herself on the other side. The change of direction is the inward journey back to Source, as the outward expansion of the universe stops and begins its collapse.

In *Planet Earth Today* we asked you to remember how slow it can be to stretch out a rubber band on your finger, hold it still while you take aim at something and then how fast it can snap back into shape as you let it fly. That's a lot like the end of the universe, the snap back into shape while moving at its fastest speed. Currently you are in the quiet of the "taking aim" phase, but it won't last much longer. You will notice increases in speed in everything soon as you all journey on the road to the end, although this will probably not happen in your own lifetimes. You are in the preliminary phase signalled by the departure of Melchior. This signals the biggest shift possible, the end of the universe, when the long exhale becomes the short, sharp in-breath.

29

A Universe of Polarity

A UNIVERSE of polarity delivers lessons to the Creator concerning balance and strife and highs and lows. In previous books we wrote about the darkness of war on Earth as the setting for some of the highest acts of courage, bravery and self sacrifice. These have been the gifts of this particular universe, although each life may not always have been pleasant to live.

Universes are as numerous as the leaves on a tree and there is not a finite number that applies to them or any other creation of the Creator Who Loves Us All. As the universes reach the end of their experiences of life they begin to align, as if the leaves on a tree branch all lined up facing the same direction so you could stack them easily. They wait like that until it is their turn to return to Source and they sit closer to each other than at any other time; and become porous with more coming and going of souls between them. When you meet people on your planet from other universes it is because your universe is sliding into alignment with its neighbours. Believe us; you have people from other universes on Earth for a host of different reasons. They are not here to harm you.

In the many universes of light, some were created to have no darkness, ever. These are universes like bright white sand, swishing and flowing without friction or hindrance. In the many universes of darkness, where the planets are sluggish and swollen with cold, there is unlikely to be a spark of light.

There are possible exceptions to every rule, even in universes. The universes of polarity have caused the greatest amount of interest and excitement. Outcomes are unpredictable and might be reversed at any time. The only way to avoid a planet turning from a settled planet of light to darkness was to enclose it in a shield of light, impenetrable to all except beings of light. Beneath their shields these hum along at a high, uniform vibration of love. They are wonderful planets, and their lessons in living with love will be of value to the Creator, but they stopped being exciting years ago. It's similar to watching a large tennis tournament like Wimbledon when there is a particularly close match taking place on one of the courts and everyone rushes to watch the excitement. Earth has been the most exciting game possible to observe, always on a knife edge, teetering back and forth, and we're still not sure how it will all end. We are hopeful for an end in light.

The most probable end for Earth is not going to be light, or dark either for that matter. In a universe of polarity Earth may end as both light and dark with one side having dominance. It will be a case of whether or not humans catch up with the rest of life here and ascend. This will happen when a critical mass of the people alive on Earth have realised that they are one with each other, one with all of life, and one with the Creator. This critical mass figure will be higher than fifty percent, but beyond that we are not specifying. Those who are not part of the group that understands and reaches ascension will not be large enough to thwart it happening. The ascension of humanity will contain enough momentum to take everyone together at once. In the beginning of your time here you never thought the task would be so hard or take so long.

This is where the exiting of the souls who inhabit ten or more bodies will start to make a difference. Many of those in this twenty-five to forty years old age group will have achieved their purpose in life and be ready to leave; they incarnated to swell the numbers on Earth and this is no longer required. Their purpose is the same as yours, to help the human soul reach ascension, and they will use their lives and deaths to do this. You will be in for a bumpy ride in the near future, and we hope that by explaining what is happening it will be easier for you. It will be a time of letting go for many of you, and we want it to be as easy as possible, whether it is your own life or that of loved ones.

It is greatly to the credit of humanity that it is so very determined to end its time here on Earth in light, and be willing to suffer to make sure it happens. We feel the suffering in your hearts when loved ones die, and how much you want to keep them alive with you. By inviting the Covid-19 virus to change the energy around death, humanity showed its seriousness and dedication to the ultimate purpose of ascension. You do not need an overwhelming number of people to die from the virus; you only need enough to change the energy. As we said, energy is changed fastest by physical actions and dying is a physical action. It is grabbing the energy of death and allowing it to run through your hands in a smooth ribbon, easy and flowing. It is only the energy that matters in every situation. At the time of writing, the Covid-19 virus is continuing its work, and when it is no longer so deadly there could well be something else following behind. The important thing is not to worry and go along with the flow of life as it is happening to you. Keep living your lives and adjust them only as necessary.

Covid-19 is a partner for you in this time period and whatever happens with the virus, whether it is to do with vaccinations, politics, or excessive deaths, it is here to create a change in direction and to challenge you. You will meet the challenge best if you are engaged and paying attention, to benefit from learning about what is happening in your countries and your world. There is more to this story than the figures for the many that have died. Creating capacity in your hearts and experiencing the emotions that are caused by death will help with what is coming next. This is not the time to be numbed by death and frozen in place; it is a time to experience all that life offers, including the death of loved ones. It is the experience of moving through grief with compassion to become a whole person, where all of your capacity to feel is strong and balanced and includes grief and joy.

30

Love is Why You are Here

THE COVID-19 virus is the great miracle of this age. It is a result of humanity bowing its head and admitting that outside help was needed to awaken hearts and to find its way as a sentient, feeling species. There is much anger and fear on this planet and although these are considered emotions they have no connection to the heart. They are from the mind as the *only* emotions that are truly derived from the heart are love and compassion. The heart is your contact point with the Creator Who Loves Us All where a cord leads from your heart to His heart. It can never be broken, only ignored. Are anger and fear aspects of love? They are not, they are born from lies and darkness. If it is not an aspect of love it comes from what you have taken into your head and interpreted in your own way, not the way of the Creator.

You as individuals are not accustomed to responding with love to actions and words in your life. It is hard for you to return love when you are being treated with hate, we see that and understand. That's why we are always standing by to offer you our help in what can seem an impossible task, to love everyone. Turning the other cheek is another way to think of this, as more than one of your great teachers has asked you to do. To return love when you are treated with hate is for your own benefit, you are the one who will have acted from your heart and you won't know if it will have an effect on another person. Each one of you who acts with an open heart is bringing through love straight from the Divine for all these other people on the Earth, both the planet and people who are starved of love.

Increasing the amount of love in circulation on Earth is the fastest way to make any changes. This raises the vibration of the greater human soul in its physical form and that will help you as a member of that soul group. It can sound like too big a job for an individual, but we have been trying to show you that your experience here on Earth is the most individual game that it is possible to design. How else do you expect to act? You don't have a hive mind like the bees, so your actions will be as individuals. In fact what we are witnessing is a determined percentage of individuals relating to each other in a more connected way. This has come about because of the challenges you face as your world burns around you. If individuals fail to connect then they will not succeed in saving the human soul. We urge you to take individual actions to love and help everyone, always doing your best and always looking for others on the same path you are on. It's time to lead the way and encourage your friends and acquaintances to join you. It's time to drop some of the barriers in your minds you put up to keep yourselves separate.

Dropping barriers in your minds has always been one of the final steps before people ascend. It was the purpose of the ancient site of Woodhenge in the UK, and that is not the only location on the planet created to make this easier. We said we were here to help you, and we created some of the sacred sites in the world to assist you. Find the Earth energy sites near you or on vacation and meditate to see how they affect you. In a site like Woodhenge it does not have to be a conscious decision to drop the barriers between the minds of the group in the circle. After a group visit you can find people finishing each other's sentences and answering questions before they are asked. It is comfortable to be like this with your friends once you let go of your fear of being too close to other people. Step by step you change and grow closer while some of you lead the way. Dropping barriers does not open your entire private mind unless you are willing for it to happen.

Another way to lower barriers is to turn the other cheek. Choose one weekend to accept all that comes your way without resentment or feeling it is a personal attack. Even your most awkward acquaintances will relax and be pleasant companions. When you withdraw from your half of any confrontation they have nothing to get hold of, no way to continue an argument. This does not mean you have to stay silent, but it is a way to find their best side in your expectations and that is the side they end up showing to you. We suggest you try it any time you are worried about meeting certain difficult people again. Love will replace aggression and unhappiness.

You live in an aggressive age, where people with vested interests are eager to keep stoking up the flames of discord. There is never a chance for peace or a time to be free of the continual stimulation by social media increasing fear and hate. It is not necessary to change your views on life if you simply back away from the continual stirring of emotions by people who benefit from the heightened feelings you hold. You will be able to settle down and remember that you are brothers and sisters together on a loved planet. Would it help if there was a worldwide blackout of the internet? It's on more than one of your possible future timelines.

Love is the reason you are here on this planet. As a soul of light you chose to work with the vibrations of light in love, joy, and truth. Some of you have always done so. What are you to make of the latest versions of your leaders driving you to hate your neighbours? The conflict between your souls and how you act in hate can tear you apart. Those who have embraced hate have had to wall up their hearts so as to stop hearing or feeling their higher selves, exactly like ignoring your conscience. It's a risky choice as a healthy heart is required to keep you alive. Those who cut off their hearts energetically have unplugged from life already. These are some of the people that Covid can help to leave the planet. If it seems a bit harsh on them, remember they are being torn apart by being a soul of light that has lost its way. It's a way to make the soul's pain stop, and let them have some peace and rest. Honour them for what they bring to you in your experience of living on Earth.

31

Challenging Times Ahead

HUMANITY has lined up for itself a series of challenges in the near future. You may have read different predictions of how many years there are left until the planet's point of no return is reached due to climate change. Forget all of those numbers; they are incomplete as they leave out too much information in their calculations. They leave out the way the energy can speed up and slow down and how it affects the rest of the world. Energy creates movement and flow, and there will be increased movement of all kinds and in different directions in your future.

The climate crisis will require you to be careful when taking steps forward and to be prepared to turn corners swiftly in the years to come. We do not say turn around and go back, as that way is closed to you now. Your future lies in unexpected directions that few can imagine right now. As it is so hard to see around corners until you have reached them, you will not anticipate each change in energy and the opportunities for progress they will bring. Added to this is the number of people on the planet, the different nations and the corners they must each reach to change direction. In all of this movement and confusion humanity will return to its one purpose and goal, that of ascension. Various actions will begin to coalesce until humanity looks like a wedge of people driving forward in unison to reach your goal. Those who choose division will not be part of this to begin with, until they die or bow to the inevitable changes. The goal is unity and remembering you are all one, there is no space there for division and hating others. There is no room for hate at all.

Focusing on your differences instead of your similarities leads to a dead end for humanity. Divisive energy is dead energy as it does not support life and increasingly leads to taking the lives of others. This is even more important now as the vibration of the Earth rises. Those who preach hate against their brothers and sisters today draw on the life force energy of their own followers and there is a limit to how long this supply of hate will be there to support them. If this planet were one of those belonging to Melchior the story would be reversed. There would be a universe full of dark energy to support fear and hate provided by his team of demons. On Earth the energy support is all of light and love to help you find the changes that lead you ever closer to joy and happiness. These are the qualities of light in the universe, embrace them and recognise what you are dealing with when you listen to people talking. You have a good representation of both light and dark present on your planet now.

Changes that are coming will continue to bring a higher death rate than you have been used to. First will be the climate crises making a number of places uninhabitable. It will drive crop failures and emigration as people become refugees in order to live. Famine will reappear in the near future, as will tensions over water access, which could spread to local fighting.

Radiation and war are a further two possibilities. There are many sources of harmful radiation, an excess burst from your Sun, nuclear accidents, careless clean up of these accidents, and deliberate acts of war and sabotage. Radiation is deadly and can cause infertility, making it a devastating weapon. It will contribute to falling birth rates.

War happens when there is a perceived weakness and an easy victory. It also happens when there is money to be made for the armaments industry or when there are scarce resources to fight over. Those instigating the wars are almost never the ones who fight in them, or their own offspring. Other people's children are considered expendable. Considering people expendable is like considering a part of your own body expendable, such as one of your hands. These leaders are not the right people to have control over your destinies. They are those who hate and seek to divide their populations so as to remain in power versus those who love and work as widely as they can to find solutions. It should be an easy choice in an election, but it isn't. Not enough people are conscious of their purpose and aware of their own possibilities. It is the job of the various crises that are coming to raise the overall level of awareness.

This is not meant to frighten you but to inform you, so you can be conscious and aware of the changes happening. Be alert, be attuned to every changing breeze like a rabbit is attuned to every smell and sound, sniffing and listening. Pay attention to the Earth changes like volcanoes and earthquakes, not blind to them, and take them seriously. We value those who are moving forward in love and we will always do what we can to help you take the right steps and weather any storm, just as when animals flee in advance of a tsunami. Know what is really important to you to move smoothly through any storm. We are guides and are able to advise you. Listen for our voices in your hearts.

32

Declining Birth Rates

THE CLIMATE crisis should be everyone's priority at this time. Every government budget and every law passed should be vetted to see if it makes the climate worse or if it improves the situation. Scientists could be diverted to finding solutions and people be employed to teach how to live with the planet, immediately. New building projects must all be eco-friendly and carbon neutral. You can think of more to add to the list, like clean methods of transport. Would you like for these suggestions to be followed everywhere and if they were, what would be the outcome? What can you see yourself doing? Choose your role and start living it now, even if you are alone in doing so. People will join you.

Failure to address the climate crisis through lack of government action and entrenched business practices goes much further than simple "head in the sand" mentality. They rely on the belief that wealth will always buy business leaders and politicians a safe haven even if many others die. This, obviously, is a lack of love for anyone but themselves. These leaders may not know any better, but we hope that you now understand that you cannot indulge in lack of love or dislike or hate for them as they are strong emotions that travel around the world creating more of the same. Feeling compassion for these people is appropriate for their inability to see others as they see themselves, along with caring for them because they are also you. You are being challenged on so many fronts these days to move forward in love, so look out for these traps that draw you into anger and lack of love. We see how hard this can be and at the same time how well many of you are doing with the challenges. If you want to progress and grow, challenge yourself! It's exactly what the greater human soul decided it had to do to succeed in this game.

One challenge is to quickly change almost everything in the way you have been accustomed to living. Covid-19 is changing the way you live with each other and do business together. Many countries are facing declining birth rates (China, Italy, Japan, etc.) and some have even been considering how to pay women to have more children. Declining birth rates are not an insurmountable problem, nor is this the first time on Earth birth rates have declined. Recently there has been steady, exponential growth in population numbers which drives continual economic growth, but in the past these numbers rose and fell repeatedly. When you are in balance with the Earth you have cycles of growth and rebirth - round and round the changes come and go, endlessly flowing and never standing still. The natural world exists in cycles and spirals. It seeks for balance in all things, whether in numbers of species, days of rain, or length of seasons. Humanity is the anomaly here, so divorced from the natural world that they are content to overrun the planet with people, even while seeing the effect it has on all the other life here. Up until now it has been beyond your ability to change or stop this pattern. There is no cosmic blame here; we can't expect you to do something you are unable to do. So what is different now?

The changes unleashed upon you currently and in the

coming years have come from one source, the greater human soul. Individual actions of free will are slowly being reined back in and safeguards are in place for the newest humans on the planet. The older residents do not have any restrictions on their behaviour and can still choose to experiment with literally anything. The post-2012 babies have inbuilt rules to help proceed towards the ascension you've all been working for. What rules have been imposed on these young people? First, love your neighbour as you love yourself. Second, if you love your neighbour as yourself you don't need any other rules. You will give to them the love you hold for yourself, and help them to find everything that is good. You don't have to wait to be reincarnated to live like this, you can start now. Begin by seeing all other people as a splinter of the same soul, just as you are yourself. It's nice to think it will be easier naturally for the young people to do this and it does not violate any contract with the Earth or anyone else.

When enough people know that they are one and treat each other with love there will be a shift in humanity. This will coincide with some people still living on Earth who haven't yet learned to love. The love vibration is high and fine, and to shift the whole population up a level into love can be seen as ascending a step on a ladder. This is not the final ascension you are hoping for, but it is how it will happen, step by step. Think of the movement and effort it takes to go up a step on a ladder and away from the ground. Consider that all the rest of life on Earth is higher up the ladder than humanity and extending a helping hand backwards, because they are living in this love vibration already. Ascending a ladder of love lifts you away from the black energy you have used to cover the Earth, that of fear, hatred and grief. It will become easier to ascend as you shake this darkness off your feet and without humanity anchoring it onto the planet these energies will disappear. You have worked incredibly hard to learn the lessons you set for yourself and you are almost, but not quite, there.

33

Stability, Not Growth

MANY governments don't have the vision to find another way of running their economies other than basing it on the eternal growth of populations and ever increasing demand for goods. It's a new challenge for them, but they are not yet considering how to tear down their old economic models (which will <u>not</u> continue to work) and build new, self-sustaining economies. Self-sustaining economies based on stable or dropping population levels will be a lighter burden on the planet and buy you some breathing space. All countries facing low birth rates should be thinking outside the box now and re-imagining how they will be run in the future. They could get a head start on what is inevitable, a slowing down of population growth and stable or dropping numbers of citizens. This isn't about the elderly that need supporting by workers; it's about how the young people will live in a balanced world.

The planets that retreated behind energy shields to wait out the end of the universe in light are stable planets. They are not battling overpopulation or a climate crisis, they do not have an emotional overload of grief or fear and they have learned to live in a sustainable fashion. This book may have given the impression that humans will ascend very soon and, following that, the Earth will immediately go through a gateway. "Immediately" in the timeless universe is a tricky concept, we recommend you instead aim to live on Earth in a stable way, having stopped the destruction and returned her to the healthy garden planet of her youth.

Stability on Earth will not be achieved while you have large numbers of refugees carrying the energy of homelessness. Homeless people in large cities also upset the planetary balance. Earth is upset by the imbalance of the humans on her surface as she struggles to provide balance to all life. You live on an unbalanced planet with the poles tipping over because of emotional overload and the lack of joy. The populations in some countries will continue to rise as refugees move around the planet and this will mask their economic problems for a short time. All forward thinking governments should be planning today for sustainability. It's an opportunity for economists to devise new blueprints for economies based on stability and not growth.

These are the years of humanity's great challenges, and as individuals we encourage you to find your way to leading others to helpful and positive solutions. We expect very few of you to flash across the world stage as a leader, but to act more in a local and family way. You are already standing on one side of a line drawn in the sand, and that line says "I'm not doing it this way anymore. There are better alternatives." And off you go to find them and tell others. With your support the cleaner, alternative products and ways of living begin to thrive until they are no longer new or non-mainstream. It will be how everyone lives. Change will come from the bottom before it comes from the top.

Go back into this book and find your starting point for change, complete one change then choose another. We are guides and you picked up this book, the information in it is meant to be topical and useable, as well as informative. It's a book about ascension for humanity and these are the jobs to be completed before that can happen. Ask us for our help!

There is nothing dearer to our hearts than helping humanity finish their game in light. You can find our messages in many places: movies, plays, stories and songs. We are very present in your world and are painting our messages large and clear. If it points towards love it is from us. If it helps you or the planet it is from us. Our messages encourage and support and never pull you down. We do not go to the dark side, as that is not our place. When you receive messages of fear or lies, especially from websites, television or newspapers, from those that try to generate negative emotions in you, walk away in love and never go back. Those messages will tear you down and make you sick. It's up to you to protect yourself from them by shutting them out and turning them off. There is nothing entertaining about lies made to manipulate and control others. You can tell them by their dark energy and the way they make you feel. Why pay attention to them and allow this energy into your minds and hearts?

You have been under emotional attack these last few years. The outpouring of hate designed to manipulate you helps to gauge how much more work is needed to change hate to love. Hate is a dead end, as we said earlier. It is only with love that you will achieve your purpose of coming to Earth at all. You need to use your discernment for everything you hear these days, including our words in this book. We have every confidence in your ability to discern the energy behind everything you hear if you stop and think about how it makes you feel. If you feel simply confused then don't act on anything until you are sure of it. We talked about critical thinking in *After We Die* and that it would not be enough to go with your feelings without considering what it is you are hearing. Humans have large brains and they are meant to be used in your own service. Your soul contains the wisdom of lifetimes to help you make sense of what you are considering, and the brain is the servant of the soul. You are bombarded with words and images. What we would really like to see is everyone shut off their devices and spend more time outside, free to be healed and instructed by nature. There is true healing in the world if you go outside and search for it.

34

The Dawn of the Endless Day

THE DAWN of the endless day refers to humanity's future as a soul of light, on a planet of light, having passed through the planetary gateway of light. This planet of polarity, of night and day, light and dark, hot and cold will continue its existence at a new, higher vibration. It will have moved away from your one Sun to the part of the universe lit by the presence of the Creator Himself, through the gateway that opens from one reality into another. At the other side of the gateway is the waiting room at the "train station" for the final journey Home. When the train of planets leaves the station for a non-stop journey back to the Creator, it will end by recombining with all of existence and becoming one with all, breathing a sigh of relief as the loneliness of separation comes to an end.

The Earth risked allowing this human game of isolation to take place on her surface in the most extreme form ever seen in the universe. Let us remind you how these living experiences usually work, some of which we already covered in *After We Die*. A soul contracts with a planet after submitting a proposal for a game of life to play that game out on her surface. This is not done in isolation from any other souls that are also present, as you can see from the relationships in a functioning ecosystem. This particular experience of many, many, many life forms on Earth included a price, set by the planet, which was that humanity would join her in

131

ascension as the end point and goal of each soul's game. This is a game with the highest price ever set by a planet in the entire universe, and Earth took on the greatest risk in hosting the human game of isolation. Humanity committed to ascension when it signed the contract, and failing to do so will put it in breach of contract.

You may be surprised to hear us speak in legal terms, but where do you think your laws come from? They have their base in Universal Law, and must not contradict these laws. If you were to pass a law that promoted murder for example, then that would be in breach of Universal Law and you could be stopped and penalised by the Governors of the universe who enforce the will of the Creator. (The Governors are His representatives in each universe who ensure that the overall plans stay on track. They are a tiny part of God, just as you are.) There is a little lee-way here, where the entire soul is not punished for the actions of a few renegade murderers. The First Universal Law is to "treat others as you wish to be treated yourself" as you are all one in relation to each other and the Creator.

Humanity originally assumed its planned role as part of the ecosystem on Earth. This changed during the time of Atlantis, when people were tempted down a pathway of darkness and destruction and tried to kill the planet itself *(The Downfall of Atlantis)*. Following the removal of Atlantis from the Earth and dispersing the survivors, there were a lot of changes. One of the main ones was that you no longer saw anything other than a three dimensional world. Gone were the angels and dark angels, elementals and any other higher dimensional beings. You could only see the animals and insects you see today. Missing so much of the planetary life and reality of existence you began to create your own stories of what humanity is doing on Earth. It's been interesting for us to watch, but rarely did you even come close to remembering why you chose to be here at all.

And yet, you made progress towards finding your Creator, even while stumbling around in the dark wearing a stronger blindfold than you ever intended to wear when you began. Recently some have begun to remember that an ecosystem exists on Earth and that you are a major part of it. That's how thoroughly the blindfold was tied on after Atlantis, as the Earth tried to find a way to cope with "the problem child" that humanity was proving itself to be. But see the difference now as you are moving swiftly on the path to remembering why you are here. You had to create the climate crisis to wake up and find where you fit into all of this, and now there are many of you who will never go back to sleep. There are also many third world residents who always knew the basis of their relationship with the Earth. It's not too late to join the pathway to the future and, instead of falling off a climate cliff, begin travelling in a new direction for everyone. There is a lot of help for you from the universe right now and it is easier to go with the direction of energy than fight against it. Ask us for our help.

If you think about the climate crisis and how it might be solved, world population is one aspect to be considered. The greater human soul is in control of population births and deaths. You grew your numbers to the point of crisis and having reached that crisis you can let the numbers fall back again. If you hear about fewer babies or shrinking population numbers, never worry that all of humanity will die out. Don't worry about deaths in the pandemic or from any other source. Humanity is adaptable and is working to reach ascension. Your role is to remember that you are all one while living on the planet and by concentrating on that you will be brought successfully to the end of your life.

Death is always a part of life; it is the final end to everyone's learning experiences before re-joining the greater human soul and remembering who you are and why you are here. Each of you remembers your purpose once you have died and regained your full consciousness before incarnating again. Very few living on the planet today have fully regained consciousness and recall the role of humans on Earth. This book contains everything you need to "wake up" and remember. Take your time absorbing the information and live like your very soul depended on your actions, because it does. Those of you who reach full consciousness while still alive on Earth are the precious holders of the energy of ascension. You stand as a light in the darkness and help those who are lost find their way to the light. You will do this without effort and without trying hard to shine; you will simply shine bright enough for all to see their way to the light. Sometimes when we are writing these books it seems that we are asking you to work hard to ascend, but the hard work is almost completed for many of you. By shining and ascending you will automatically no longer wish to do the things that hint at darkness, instead you will always be looking for the straight pathway to the light and have no trouble seeing it right before your feet. You will lead and others will observe you and follow. All you will be doing is being true to yourself, your purpose and your heart.

35

Separation and Mental Health

YOUR long game of wearing a blindfold has resulted in an extended series of individual incarnations taking place in isolation from your soul group. Imagine if the cells inside your body could not communicate with each other or work together as one. Humanity has been incarnating over and over again and we feel we are seeing soul loneliness take its toll on mental health, along with the other causes mentioned in the media. Very few people these days seem not to have some sort of mental health problems; people are so damaged mentally that the depth of the illness can only be identified when it has reached an extremely high level. How did this evolve into such a problem?

The game of isolation designed by you for living on Earth was to discover how far you could remove yourself from the Creator Who Loves Us All, then once that was in place find yourself again as a tiny part of God. By doing this you would explore the effects of being isolated from the vast reservoir of love present in the universe. This love binds all together in oneness, harmony, beauty and peace. You have little idea on Earth of the real force of this love as it exists beyond your home planet. You have been isolated from it while learning about the depths of separation. Your choice was to experience separateness and isolation, and then take the lessons learned back to the Creator at the final end of the universe. While we applauded your bravery none of us wanted to be in your shoes when you chose to live in this very unnatural, lonely and confusing manner. Love, along with the universal community of souls supports each of us in our own roles.

One unique addition to humanity's game included being separate individual souls from each other in death as well as life. Therefore, you did not share lessons learned during your lifetimes with other human souls while waiting for your next incarnation. This is unique among soul groups and slowed you down considerably. Other souls, such as dogs, share all their life experiences with each other when they meet between lives.

Humanity was also unable to fit into the patterns formed by the other residents on the planet, such as animals and insects, fish and birds, etc. These other soul groups were busy creating systems that allowed them to live in balance with each other, the plants, water and earth. Even with so many separate soul groups on one planet they continued to live by the lessons of the outer universe and applied them to their communities, forming functioning ecosystems. They do very well when allowed to exist undisturbed. They live their lives and some die to provide food so others may live; they pollinate plants and spread seeds for future generations to eat and to provide natural homes. Each takes only what they need and no more. They do this also to help humanity, in spite of so many of you disregarding their gifts to you.

The universe exists as a large support network for all life everywhere. It is the structure that allows you to make plans by knowing the boundaries of those plans, within the limits that are set by universal law. Without boundaries and structure, you would not have an increased flow of light and you would have variable answers to any one question, causing confusion. Planetary games are very precisely designed to stay within boundaries and deliver an experience. If it is desired to vary the experience a whole new planetary game can be started after the current one is finished. It is not helpful for anyone to confuse their learning experiences by not having an idea of what the goal is or how it will be achieved. Free will exists within these set boundaries, as does everything that has happened on Earth. It's what you do that is unexpected and new within these games that teach everyone a little more about what it is to be a part of the Divine.

You were deliberately isolated from the universe until 2013, when the shell surrounding Earth began to break up. Once that happened the energy of love and support, along with other universal energies were no longer blocked from the planet. For the first time in eons the Earth and her inhabitants were exposed to these outside influences. They provide a balancing effect for everyone. The balancing energy you need on Earth is unconditional love and it is in such short supply that people have been sliding into hate, and feeling justified in doing so. Grief, fear, hatred are all on the ascendant because there is a shortage of compassion. The universe is built on compassion and it is the universal life force energy that was used in the creation of the universe, it is the energy of pure, unconditional love. Every human has the right to be loved. If you are a healer, and this is the foundation of the practice of Reiki (universal life force energy), then you are channelling this universal love to heal yourself and others from the effects of living with insufficient love. Reiki and other healing modalities bridge the barriers between Earth and the universe and brings through this purest of energies to nourish and balance the terrible lack of love. This is why it is necessary to use your healing skills regularly once you are taught or initiated in them.

You may feel everything is getting less and less balanced these days and the reason for this is not due to the lack of love and support, but to the way everyone was before 2013. Since then many have been open and able to receive the energy, becoming softened and looking up to the stars. These people became more cognizant of those around them. For some others, nothing can get through their hard outer shells and they do not change. The energy of love has the ability to flow around you and through you and give you what you need to thrive. Those with hardened hearts and hard shells do not have the energy of love flowing through them, and may be impervious to the love flowing around them. This is why you need to sharpen your own perception of cause and effect. The energy of love (cause) will change people's words and actions (effect). Look for kindness and compassion to recognise who is touched by love.

Your lack of sight due to wearing a blindfold has kept you from seeing the many angels and demons that have vied for your attention. This has isolated you from reliable guidance and you are dependent on others who practice channelling to pass on the messages that we wish to share with humanity. There was a time when we walked with you and spoke directly to you in conversation. The Atlantean fiasco put an end to that. By closing off the sight and sound of angels we were also able to close off the dark angels (demons) and hinder many of their power plays. Angels work differently depending on our light and dark roles. But you were more isolated than you had originally intended at the planning stages of your living experience on Earth. Today much of that is changing and many more can see and hear us, now it is down to self-confidence and practice to tune into us. Until then we write books and movie scripts through those people who can hear or be inspired by our words.

Life on Earth has been a long experiment with individualism, leading to broken people. The extended experiment into individualism since the Second World War has led to gains in understanding the nature of humanity and the mental state of society. You could "have it all" and make choices of how you wanted to live as an individual, no longer required to follow in a parent's footsteps. A change has arrived since the millennium in the understanding of the young that it is only in collective action humanity can achieve anything. The experiment of individualism ran long enough to show that you can't survive as individuals. The failure of individualism is apparent in the society-wide decline in mental health and human development. You've been asked to do everything on your own and this leaves people behind. The big names in business, sports and entertainment have huge pyramids of people supporting their success.

Were you isolated enough to learn everything you needed to learn in this manner? Perhaps not, because for much of 2020 and 2021 many people in the world became even more isolated in their own homes from a variety of national lockdowns and stay-at-home orders due to Covid-19. The issue of mental health has been highlighted by this extreme separation and division of millions of people. Countries were isolated with their borders shut, dividing many families. Inside these countries movement was restricted and regulated, keeping families, friends and co-workers apart. We don't see how you can take isolation any further, but the main question to ask surrounding separation is: how's the mental health situation? What has isolation and separation done to people's ability to function as human beings? You only need to look at current divisive behaviour and listen to people's stories to learn the answers to this question. From our point of view, separation and isolation drives you crazy.

Will this experience be enough for you to begin looking at each other and see your common humanity, or will you find even more ways to separate? The comfort and pleasure in life can be other people who love you and see you for the unique and special person you are. It can also be many other things, but as your goal is to remember you are all one, it can help to be with not just your usual companions, but as great a variety of people as you can manage to meet. Make links and form bonds with others. If you befriend someone outside your comfort zone, they will probably turn and befriend someone else. It works as a way to make the connections you need to move beyond isolation and separation. If you have had enough isolation to last you a lifetime, take positive steps to end it. Living is what you are here for and ascension is on the other side of separation.

In the past we've talked about a pendulum that has swung as far as it can go in one direction before it can begin heading back. You are nearly there now. Your actions to end isolation are a factor in deciding whether the pendulum is ready to swing back or not. Actions create energy and you may as well be the one leading the way forward in love, as opposed to those who wish to promote separation from others they hate. Allow the future to arrive.

Books by Candace Caddick

In 2009 the Archangels wanted to write a channelled book about the Earth and help us to see the reality of the world we live on. Planet Earth Today shows a sentient planet of incredible beauty, and a human soul of light. I channelled this book by six Archangels, which was a combination of them explaining while I asked questions. Planet Earth Today is the first of a set of seven books that the Archangelic Collective wrote about the coming years. The contents of their books are always relevant to what is happening now and lead decades into the future.

There is a single story of humanity, a golden book like a long scroll and the books have been taken from here and typed up. I felt that as long as I was learning new information when writing, information that I couldn't begin to make up, I was on track as an accurate channel. I watched the flow of golden words enter the computer each time until it was the last page of each book. After that my daughter and I checked and checked that I had written it correctly, each paragraph and line examined to see if the golden energy ran through it steadily or if it wavered indicating that it was not quite accurate. Only when we were happy was a section considered complete. Later sometimes I would add more clarity to a section, as my own understanding improved and I could put in more detail. I channel using a combination of sound and sight, and where it is written the best I have been writing down their exact words.

Planet Earth Today

This first book gives background information on the roles played in the universe by the Earth and the greater human soul. Life is experienced so as to learn why each is alive to know themselves. Humanity wished to live on Earth wearing a blindfold and they could neither see the higher dimensions nor connect to their over-arching human soul. This has led to great loneliness and separation as we began to play the hardest game ever conceived. The Archangel of Darkness presents his point of view of humanity on Earth, and the Archangels of Light: Ariel, Esmariel the Archangel of Transformation, and Hophriel the Archangel of Hope, write with techniques to take you forward with hope.

This book serves as the introduction as it takes place before the other books in time, and the information about the planet or Atlantis is not repeated in any other book. However, each book stands alone and can be read individually.

ISBN 978-0-9565009-0-8

The Downfall of Atlantis

In the story of humanity on Earth, the time spent living and learning in Atlantis cannot be ignored. During those long years darkness gathered around human beings, and science developed a heartless approach. There were slaves made of combined people and animals, and ultimately, cloning was used to keep the wealthy and powerful alive indefinitely. Cloning was the final crack in the system that led to ruin and the destruction of Atlantis.

Those who refused to go along with the new science escaped Atlantis in the final days and settled on the surrounding land masses, forming the new post-Atlantean civilisations. The Atlantean influence on the cultures of Africa, Egypt, Britain and Celtic Europe, North, Central and South America is explored. They learned much from the local residents in return.

Atlantean civilisation remained intact for a long time in Britain because of the ancient power sites at Avebury, Stonehenge and Glastonbury Tor. When the Shadow in the East pushed westwards into Europe the light of these venerable societies vanished, until only King Arthur and Merlin were left to protect the Earth from darkness. Their story explains the true significance of the great stone circles, and how we came to forget the real story of Arthur and the sacrifices he made to destroy the invading armies. The connection in a straight line between Atlantis, post-Atlantean civilisations, King Arthur and the Time of Legends is explored so we can remember those things we have forgotten, and not repeat past mistakes.

ISBN 978-0-9565009-1-5

And I Saw A New Earth

Humanity is entering its golden years, when you begin to live as you always intended when you came to Earth. It will be like breathing for the first time, the sweet fresh air that is real life filled with joy, truth and clear-sightedness. And I Saw A New Earth is a channelled book about light, written by those who have ascended in wisdom and understanding and wish to help during a time of rapid change.

During 2012 the Earth received wave after wave of light, enough light to change the way you relate to each other, enough light to show you the lies that have kept you from living in joy. By December the rebirth of Earth herself took place filled with the energy of Spring and fresh beginnings. Humanity can take this energy forward to remove failing institutions and restore the balance between work and play. 2012 changed the energy of the world you know: one of gross inequality and lack of hope. The coming years give you the chance to build societies of love and fairness, leaving behind the institutions that failed you.

And I Saw a New Earth is written to reassure you that you can trust your intuition and your hearts, and that your real future lies ahead for you to enjoy. Humanity has one of the most important roles in the future of the universe.

ISBN: 978-0-9565009-2-2

Guidebook to the Future

There are an overwhelming number of changes taking place in the coming years. It's as if you began a long journey without a map where the road, even the destination, keeps changing while you travel. As soon as you become accustomed to one change another one takes its place. It's the beginning of the new 26,000 year galactic cycle and of the new Earth. Changes are taking place in the higher dimensions that will affect your society and economies and influence the forward progress of humanity. Think of this book as a map or guidebook into the future, showing you the new energy and how it shapes your individual pathways. We want you to relax, let go and enjoy the journey.

Angels are beings of love and light, and this book was channelled to help people look past the radical new changes to the happier world beyond.

ISBN: 978-0-9565009-3-9

Stepping Through the Looking Glass

This book helps us discover what it is to leave the old world behind and step ahead into the new. We no longer live on the same planet energetically; we are stepping through the looking glass onto a new Earth where we are more aware of the higher dimensions and magic of existence.

The energy on Earth today supports not only change but also finding and making those changes; it does not support the continued patterns of our old ways of living. It's as if a light bulb has come on in a room and we can see clearly, where before a major part of the circuitry of our world was missing. Now the circuit is complete again. The battery has been plugged back in and is filling the world with energy, where we had been running on only the memory of that energy.

This book takes us through the parallels between our time and ancient Egypt, concentrating on the impact made on life by the Atlantean survivors. The Archangels include chapters on magic, to help us break free of out-of-date limitations through understanding and practice. A change has taken place in the way the greater human soul intends to use death. Death can be a tool for consolidation and a splintered soul can become stronger by retiring some souls from the planet while others continue to incarnate.

And finally, there is more help on the way as humanity pulls out all the stops to bring through new waves of advanced souls to assist us. It's the beginning of a new future where we mean to succeed and achieve our own ascension.

Writing this book, they would say "more about death, more about magic!" until all the information was included the text.

ISBN: 978-0-9565009-4-6

After We Die

"Your soul flows like a ribbon through the universe, meeting people here, then twisting and flowing away to join others over there; a ribbon of golden energy touching the lives of other people. You touch down lightly and absorb knowledge, then lift and flow away. Others are doing the same and your paths cross many times, making elegant woven patterns of light. Life moves effortlessly and you find yourself always in the right place with the right companions. What at first seems unplanned and pointless always happens exactly as it should. Then you are born into a body." Archangel Azrael

The Archangel Azrael writes about death with love and compassion for all who have forgotten what waits on the other side of the veil. At a time when everything is changing for us, he explains what is happening and why it is happening now, and the importance of using death to balance and complete life. In the past this was information known by all, but once it was forgotten, the fear of death and confusion around the afterlife became entrenched. Angels would see us live in love and happiness and accept our end with peaceful hearts.

Azrael completes the book with more information about star beings, why the young are becoming gender fluid, crop circles, global economics, a decline in population numbers and Earth changes. There are exercises to assist in balancing your energy and how to discern truth from lies, and what to do when you've found the truth. This book introduces the final stage for humanity as it ascends and begins its journey back to the Creator Who Loves Us All as part of the Earth's new Mega-Soul.

ISBN 978-0-9565009-5-3

Dawn of the Endless Day

This book is about the ascension of the human soul. For many years individual souls have endeavoured to remember who they are and why they are here; what is the meaning of life and does God exist? People are beginning to remember that they are here on a mission - to know who they are - souls that embody love.

The Earth has a plan for her future, where she is a planet of light combining with all the souls of light for whom she has provided a home. This is the point where she shifts into her next phase and the stellar gateway opens. On the other side of the gateway she joins those planets who are readying for their final return to the Creator Who Loves Us All.

How does humanity fit in to this planetary story? Are you all ready to make the transition to light in her company? Every action holds energy. This book is filled with practical steps for individual actions, ones that can change the energy of the entire human race. As small streams feed into a river, individual changes create the flow to return the planet to a healthy state.

This book is written by the Archangel Melchizadek who teaches us to live by the universal laws taught to us so long ago. "Treat everyone as you wish to be treated yourself." "Love thy neighbour as you love yourself." "Put the planet back the way you found it." These few rules will see humanity step over the threshold into the new Dawn of the Endless Day.

ISBN 978-0-9565009-6-0

About the Author

I am a teaching Reiki Master who studied for ten years with my Master, prior to initiation in the Usui Shiki Ryoho system of Reiki. Since 1993 I have been practicing my own Reiki daily and my ability to channel has become clearer and stronger until a few years ago I realised I was able to see the world around me in a way that others did not. My efforts, as I worked with my own archangelic guides as a channel, were always to unblock and deliver the message clearly, with no preconceptions of what they may say next; to stand well back and just watch and listen.

Before learning Reiki I trained as an economist, worked inside the United States Congress in Washington D.C. as a legislative assistant, and retrained as a nutritionist in the UK.

If you want to read more from the Archangels and other beings of light, I write a regular channelled blog at:

www.candacecaddick.com

Printed in Great Britain
by Amazon

85424965R00099